Caught by Alaska!

Jack Jeffrey

with a Foreword by

Bob DeArmond

I hope you will enjoy my true Alaska Stories

Jack Jeffrey

Hara Publishing

Published by
Hara Publishing
P.O. Box 19732
Seattle, WA 98109
(425) 775-7868

ISBN: 1-883697-81-6

Library of Congress Number 2001089613

Manufactured in the United States
10 9 8 7 6 5 4 3 2

Typography and Design: Stephen Herold of Books AtoZ

Jack Jeffrey

TABLE OF CONTENTS

PT. BARROW
WAINWRIGHT
KOTZEBUE
KOYUKUK R.
NOME
UNALAKLEET
YUKON RIVER
McGRATH
KUSKOKWIM R.
NUSHAGAK R.
MULCHATNA R.
BETHEL
KONGIGANAK
KWIGILLINGOK
EKWOK
LAKE ILIAMNA
COOK INLET
DILLINGHAM
BRISTOL BAY
GULF
KODIAK I.
ATTU I.
KISKA
ALEUTIAN IS

N A D A

Sites in Alaska
mentioned in
the stories

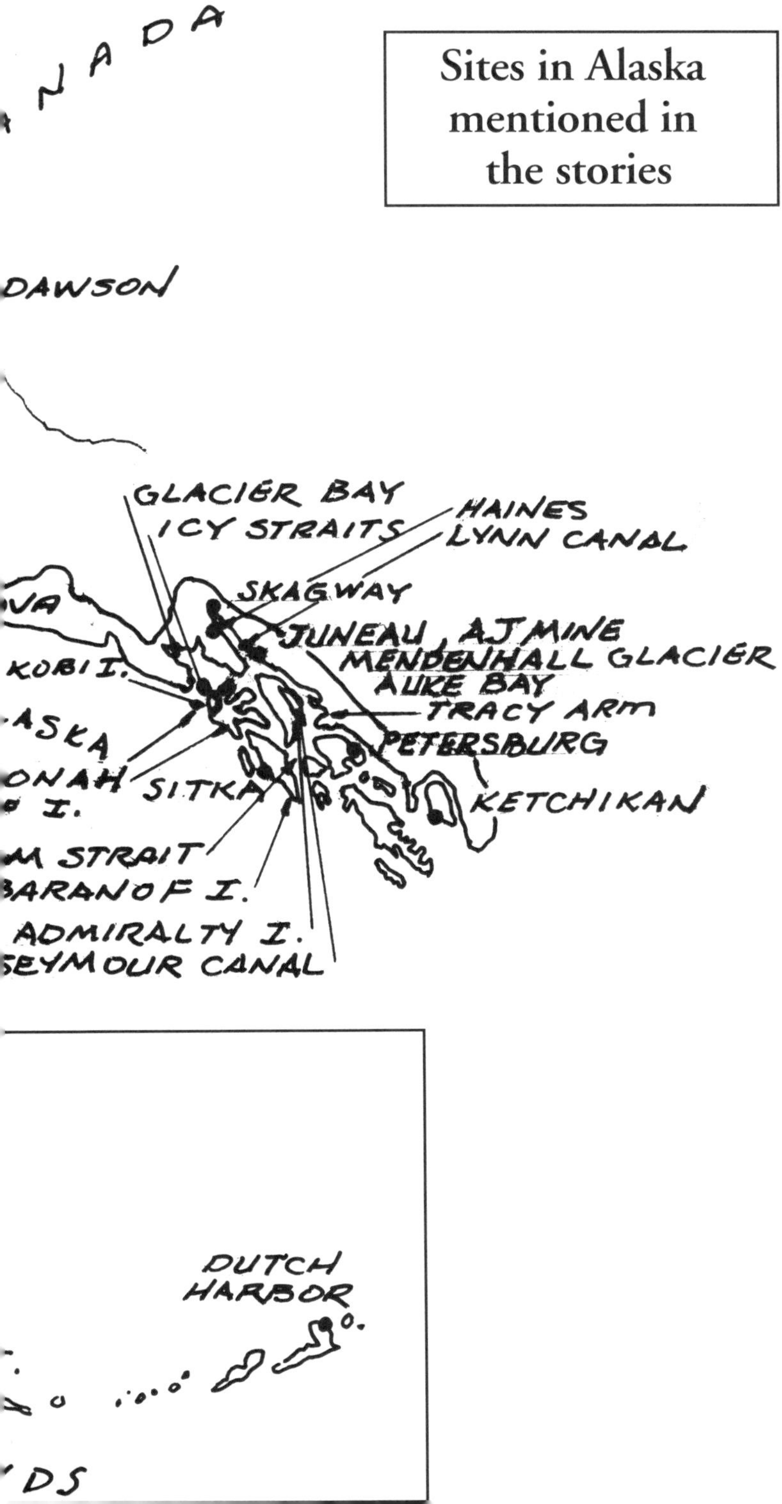

DAWSON

GLACIER BAY
ICY STRAITS
HAINES
LYNN CANAL

SKAGWAY

JUNEAU , AJ MINE
MENDENHALL GLACIER
AUKE BAY
TRACY ARM
PETERSBURG

KOBI I.

VA

ASKA

ONAH
I.

SITKA

KETCHIKAN

M STRAIT
BARANOF I.
ADMIRALTY I.
SEYMOUR CANAL

DUTCH
HARBOR

DS

INTRODUCTION

My father's stories were a regular occurrence at our family home in Seward, Alaska. At the time, I thought all fathers were the same and had wonderful, adventurous stories to tell. It wasn't until later in life that I realized Dad had a special talent, had lived quite a different kind of life, and had an amazing ability to mesmerize any listener.

When Dad retired, he began typing the stories in the way that he told them. He hoped that this might serve his family well with a recorded "oral history" of not only his adventures and life, but of an Alaska that does not exist anymore.

My children and I received several stories a month for a number of years. Dad's grandchildren, Jeff and Jennie, recall coming home and automatically glancing at the kitchen table to see if another story had arrived. Dinners were always more fun and interesting if we had a good story to read during dessert. Soon, these stories were being shared with friends. And, friends were sharing stories with other friends. Various Alaskan magazines printed his stories.

It was after the fortieth story arrived at my home that a good friend, Janice Murphy, showed Gladi Kulp of the Alaska State Library in Juneau some of these stories. At this point, it seemed that the stories had a life of their own. Many thanks to Gladi for her belief that these stories represented not only a unique time in Alaska, but also a special way of life. On November 1, 1996, all of Jack Jeffrey's Alaskan stories became a part of the Alaska Historical Collection in the Alaska State Library. We were all happy that Dad's stories were now available for many more people to enjoy.

Yet, Bo Miller, my husband, believed strongly that these stories should be published. Many thanks to our daughter, April Miller, for her astute comments and ideas in revising some of the writing. While I typed night after night, Bo began scrutinizing old black and white photos in family albums with a magnifying glass. These old photos, plus the kind donation of three more photos from the Alaska State Library, led to the completion of the book.

I think one of the most exciting times of all during this process was when Bob DeArmond called from Sitka to tell us that he would gladly write the foreword. I had met Bob briefly on a visit to the Pioneer Home in Sitka while retracing my family's roots. It is a great honor for Bob to give of himself in this manner.

Completing circles of life and friendships seem to be a recurring theme while putting together this book. It became obvious that the cover needed an Alaskan scene and we gathered together many ideas, but none seemed suitable. One week before completion, I found myself rummaging through an unnamed box in the basement and out popped an envelope. This envelope contained a lovely water color painting of the road by Gastineau Channel by Gen Harmon, my parents' longest and dearest friend in Juneau. Not only is Gen mentioned in a story in this book, but her husband, Hank, was Dad's closest friend. Our cover was now complete.

Most of all, thanks Dad, for your sense of spirit, adventure, and love of people. I truly hope that you, the reader, come away from this book with the understanding that Alaska was, and still is, the "last frontier."

Jo Jeffrey

FOREWORD

I T WAS July 4, 1935, when nineteen-year-old Jack Jeffrey and a companion hopped a freight train in drought-stricken North Dakota and headed west. Three weeks later he was a mucker, underground in the Alaska Juneau gold mine at Juneau. In the meanwhile the two boys had lived in Seattle for ten days on two-bits a day, hoarding their cash for $8 steerage tickets to Ketchikan. They were so ignorant of Alaska that they first asked about a steamboat passage to Dawson.

They found no jobs in Ketchikan and after they had slept on the concrete floor of the jail a few nights, kindly Bill Brown, the Alaska Steamship Company agent, loaned them the price of steerage tickets to Juneau where work was more plentiful. Later it was Sitka and then Seward.

Jack Jeffrey remained twenty-five years in Alaska, but although he didn't know it when he arrived in 1935, or perhaps even when he left in 1960, he got in on the last years of what many are now calling "the good old Alaska." Alaska had about 135,000 people in 1935, scattered from Dixon Entrance to the Arctic Ocean. And by and large, partly because there were fewer of them, people from the various towns were better acquainted with each other than they are today. That was because travel to and from Alaska, and between the coastal towns, was by steamboat.

Alaskans went "down below," which means to Seattle and points beyond, by steamboat, and they returned home the same way. Depending upon where one boarded or disembarked, a traveler spent from three to ten days aboard the boat, visiting with other Alaskans, eating, dancing, playing cards, getting acquainted.

Even after they left Alaska for good, Alaskans enjoyed each other's company in such organizations as the Alaska-Yukon Pioneers, the

Ladies of the Golden North, and The Alaskans, and got together now and then for Sourdough Reunions.

Jack Jeffrey tells a great deal about that Old Alaska in this book and a reading of it will bring back memories for many an Old Timer.

Bob DeArmond
Alaskan since 1911

COMING TO ALASKA

PART ONE: A LOAN
North Dakota-Seattle-Ketchikan-Juneau, 1935

I T WAS at a picnic during the summer of 1996, as we sat talking with our good friends Betty Lee and Doug Griggs, that my thoughts became flooded with memories of another time. The story goes back to how I got to Alaska.

I graduated from Williston High School in 1933 when North Dakota was at the bottom of the Depression and drought. I believe 99 percent of the people were unemployed. Farmers could no longer get their seed back from their spring planting and farms were being deserted or sold off to big landowner companies. The picture was bleak.

At this same time, I attended the University of North Dakota for one year but ran out of money. Much to my surprise, the Montgomery Ward retail store in my hometown hired me in June 1934 as a shipping and receiving clerk. Including a very long Saturday from 7:30 A.M. to 9:30 P.M. and helping dress windows on Wednesday night, I averaged sixty-two hours a week. At about $1.17 per day. I have often been asked, "Why did you leave your hometown?" or "Why didn't you finish college?" I think it's obvious.

On July 4, 1935, my buddy Bill Trumbo and I climbed on a freight train in Williston, North Dakota, and headed for Alaska via Seattle. We were both nineteen years old. Things were bound to be better somewhere else.

I believe I had almost $15 and Bill had possibly $11. In Seattle we found out the only way that one could get to Alaska was via the Alaska Steamship's freight and passenger ships or bum a ride in a fishing boat. Alaska Steamship Company had a ticket office uptown. We applied for a ticket to Alaska.

The ticket agent asked, "Where to in Alaska?"

I said, "Dawson."

It was then that I learned that Dawson wasn't even in Alaska. Dawson was in the Canadian Yukon Territory, and a long ways from salt water.

"How about Nome?" I asked.

The agent said, "Boys, let's do it the easy way. How much money do you have?" I believe the steerage fare to Ketchikan was around $8 each, which left us about $5.50.

S.S. Yukon *sailing by the Alaskan glaciers. Photo is from about the time of this story.*

Our ship, the *S.S. Yukon,* didn't sail for ten days. We obviously had to watch our expenditures! A café called Rafferty's saved our life. It was an "all-you-can-eat" bill for 25 cents. By sleeping in vacant lots, using cardboard and newspapers for blankets, and eating one meal a day — we got by on $2.50 for the ten days and had about $3 left over on sailing day.

Our bunks were on the number two level between decks and we were also served three meals per day. We even had real blankets. Things seemed great and exciting. The ship's passengers consisted of passengers going back home to Alaska and tourists who had money, even during the

Depression. The tourists were elderly people and about half of them had a teenage granddaughter along. There were no teenage males. They must have stayed home to work.

The second day the mate came down into the hold, cornered five of us young guys, and asked, "Can you dance? Do you know how to behave yourselves? If so, clean up and be in the 'after-club' room at 8:00 P.M. We have a bunch of bored young ladies that you can help us entertain."

Most of the steerage passengers were cannery workers. The majority of them were Chinese or from the Philippines. We had a grand time. An added bonus was the evening snack about 10:00 P.M. Wow, did they serve great food!

We arrived in Ketchikan, "land where the streets are paved with gold," to seek our fortune at 8 A.M. We went ashore after gorging ourselves on the last breakfast provided. Experience had taught us to eat all that we could, for most likely it would be a long time until the next meal. We doubted that the $1.25 between us would last very long.

The streets around the waterfront were on piling and planked. Further back on land, the streets were not even paved—let alone with gold. Ketchikan had an arch over the street leading off the docks that read, "The Salmon Capital of the World." Unfortunately, the big run of salmon had not started, and the entire economy was on hold. Employment was at a low. The locals held all of the jobs, leaving the strangers with the short end of things.

By 7:00 P.M. we had covered the town and explored all known job opportunities. Canneries were busy getting ready for the canning season with maintenance crews, but no new hires. We couldn't even find a dishwashing job without paying for meals. In the year 1935, you either had a job with all of its advantages, or you were out of luck. There were no refuges for the needy. Soup kitchens were unknown in Ketchikan, welfare was unheard of, and so it went.

Ketchikan has an extremely rainy climate that made it tough for sleeping outside. The police station seemed to be the logical place to start.

"Sorry, boys," we were told. "We don't even have room for our prisoners. Why don't you try the federal jail?"

The night jailer was on duty but didn't know whether he should let us in. We finally talked him into calling the marshal who permitted us to sleep in the chicken coop. This was a lean-to building, an abandoned jail not even suitable for prisoners in those days. And it was here that we slept for the next ten nights. It was grim. There were no bunks, no mattresses, and no heat. It was just a fairly large room with a concrete floor. The jail wouldn't feed us, so we lived on old bakery goods.

In the meantime, we attempted to stow away on every ship that came in heading north without luck. Let's face it, a North Dakota kid knows little about ships and how to sneak aboard and hide.

Consequently, some days after our arrival, we were told to see the marshal who said, "I received a call from The Alaska Steamship Company's General Agent. It seems as though you boys are giving him a difficult time. He wants to talk with you."

This was sort of scary because the one thing strangers should not do is to give the local people a bad time. Gosh, we didn't realize that we were making his job difficult. In fact, we didn't even know him. We were definitely a couple of uneasy boys who entered the steamship company office and asked for Mr. Bill Brown.

Right off Mr. Brown said, "Hello, boys! So, you're the ones who have been trying to stow away on every northbound ship. We've had to put on extra gangplank watches and search each vessel before departure to keep you two from stowing away. Don't you know it's a federal offense and that you could be put in jail?"

I thought, Hey, that wouldn't be so tough.

Mr. Brown went on. "Where do you boys want to go and what do you want to do?"

We didn't know enough about Alaska to name an area that might be promising and we explained that all we wanted was a steady job so that we could live in Alaska. In the meantime, we would settle for anything.

His suggestion was that we go to Juneau. He told us that there was a great deal of new work there, such as completion of the new Federal Building and the Juneau-Douglas Bridge. City streets were being paved and there was always the Alaska Juneau Gold Mining Company that employed almost 1,000 men. This sounded great, since we had worked on paving gangs back home.

"Yes, sure!" we agreed. "But how in the heck do we get to Juneau when all we have left is 25 cents?"

4

"Well, boys," said Mr. Brown, "I'll loan you the money for two steerage tickets to Juneau."

Wow! Imagine that! A total stranger offered to loan us money. I was wearing a watch that was my high school graduation gift and I offered it as collateral.

"No," he said, "I don't want your watch. I'd only have to go to the trouble of mailing it back to you when you get enough money ahead to repay me."

So, Mr. Bill Brown took pity on us and loaned us $7.50 each for the passage from Ketchikan to Juneau. It was quite an emotional thing for us. We were accustomed to being kicked around, chased out, and yelled at. Being helped was new and difficult to handle. I had to turn away until I could control my tears.

The *S.S. Yukon* departed for Ketchikan the next day with us aboard for its twenty-four-hour run to Juneau via Wrangell and Petersburg. We spent the majority of the twenty-four hours eating and sleeping. The food was outstanding, and so much of it! The bunks, after a concrete floor, were heavenly. It was with reluctance that we went ashore the next morning in Juneau.

Two years later, in the fall of 1937, there came a knock at our apartment door. I was now married, working as a contract miner for the A.J. Mine, and an established member of the community. Ann was busy in the kitchen preparing dinner, so I went to the door. There stood someone with a familiar face.

Oh, my gosh, I thought, it's the Alaska Steamship agent from Ketchikan. I almost slammed the door shut.

My mind raced back to 1935. I was sure that I had saved my money and repaid him. Why, I even sent him a box of cigars along with the money. At least I had intended on doing it. It couldn't be the amount of the money. It must be the principle of the thing. Why else would he be here? What an ungrateful person I am. But, I'm positive that I sent him the money.

These thoughts were whirling through my head, but outwardly, I was calm and cool and said, "Can I help you?"

He replied, "Are you the young fellow who married Ann Boyer? If so, I'm an old friend of hers. She and my daughter, Betty Lee, were close friends and we just dropped by to say hello."

When Ann saw who it was, she ran to him and they hugged and kissed. I could see that they were truly happy to see one another. He stayed to dinner and they laughed and chatted about family and friends. By dessert time, I was sure of myself and broached the subject that was heavy on my mind. Would you believe it, he didn't remember me or the incident.

All he said was, "Jack, I don't remember, but if I did loan you the money, I'm certainly happy that I did."

The subject was closed for him, but I have never forgotten.

Later on, I met Bill Brown's wife, Bessie Brown, and told her my story. She said, "Oh, Bill did that all of the time. He never took down names and had no idea how much money he loaned to young men. Almost every mail-boat brought envelopes from Juneau, Anchorage, Nome, Chicago, and faraway places. Out of the envelopes would fall money and a note of thanks from young men Bill had befriended. Often, the note would say how sorry they were that it had taken so long to repay him but times had been tough."

More often than you could imagine, I have contemplated the luck or fate that resulted in my traveling to Juneau and marrying Ann, and along the way, making the acquaintance of Bill Brown and his family. Incidentally, he was later instrumental in my being employed with the Alaska Steamship Company. During the war, we attended the wedding of Betty Lee Brown to a naval officer, Doug Griggs. We maintained a happy, friendly relationship with these dear people through all of the years. Again, I say it is truly unusual that I should be at this picnic with these close friends.

PART TWO: DYNAMITE!
Juneau, 1935

WALKING UP FRANKLIN STREET in Juneau from the old Alaska Steamship dock, we passed a nice old guy with a two-day-old beard, woolen trousers, wool shirt, and hip-boots. He gave us both a big "Hello, boys!" We figured the old guy had us mixed up with some of the local boys. He turned out to be Governor Troy, the current governor of Alaska. That is the kind of welcome we received in Juneau and that is the way we found Juneau to be all of the time that we lived there. We loved it!

The downtown streets were being paved. The steel was down and they were about ready to pour on the streets around the Goldstein building. Somehow, I got hired on that morning at 8:00 A.M. Coming north, we had met Bill Roberts, a mining student at the University of Washington. Bill already had a job at the A.J. Mine. Therefore, with the mine as our goal, Bill Trumbo and I ran down to the mine office at noon and signed up. We had the entire lunch hour to fill out the forms because we didn't have any money for food.

My mining application showed that I was from North Dakota and had gone to work in the coal mines after graduating from the eighth grade. I then continued to expand my application to look the best that it could for hiring, I thought. I'd heard that it was against the law to work underground unless you were twenty-one years old, so I was, of course, twenty-two years old on the application. I also hoped that my bulk supplemented by extra shirts and a sweater would further tip the scale toward my being hired. On the negative side, I couldn't help but notice the fifty to seventy-five men looking for work. Every day a hiring list was posted on the bulletin board. It was to be checked every day. Even being an eternal optimist, I found my hopes dimmed somewhat. That night we slept on the floor of Bill Robert's room at the Alaskan Hotel.

The next morning, my partner, Bill, came running up to the paving job and yelled over the noise. "Your name is on the hiring list!"

He had gone into the office and told them to keep the job open until lunch time. At the noon break I talked to the boss and he agreed to give Bill my job and I moved over to the mining company. In less than thirty-six hours we were both employed. Bill stayed with the paving gang until he got a truck driving job. In fact, he dumped the last truckload of rock on the Douglas approach to the bridge making it possible to drive across the Juneau-Douglas Bridge. This must have been about the first week in September 1935.

I signed up with the A.J. Mine and was asked, "Where do you want to work, kid?"

"In the mine," was my reply.

Jack at the mine entrance.

I got a "Good for you, kid!"

I found out later that this particular man was Bill Redling and that he would soon become a general in the U.S. Army. I also found out later that the employment office wasn't fooled by my coal mining experience and the story of only having graduated from the eighth grade — I had worn my high school football letterman's sweater when I signed up. They hired me because of my brass, and because I was from North Dakota. They preferred to not hire city people. And their thinking was that in those times, anyone having survived and escaped North Dakota was a good hire.

So I went to work on July 25, 1935, on day shift as a mucker in the ditch at Six Cone for the Alaska-Juneau Gold Mining Company mine, better known as the A.J. Mine. The actual mine was back inside Mount Roberts. As a passenger ship rounded the rock dump at Juneau, the tourists always exclaimed, "There's the mine!" meaning the A.J. Mine but, of course, they were wrong. It was really the mill that they saw.

The mine was reached via the four-level haulage tunnel that went through a small portion of the side hill and came out again in Gold Creek Canyon, where the Alaska-Juneau camp was. At the camp were the boarding houses, steel shop (drill steel), various small-gauge railroad repair sections, and the huge air compressors. From the A.J. camp, the tunnel headed into the mountain, never to come out. This was no two-bit, fly-by-night operation. It operated on three shifts and the amount of ore mined and processed in twenty-four hours was unbelievable. As I recall, on day shift, due to traffic, it only averaged eight ore trains per shift. Swing shift, or afternoon shift, averaged eleven to twelve ore trains. Graveyard shifts did up to fifteen per hour. Each train had forty cars. Each car hauled ten tons of ore. Quickly, that runs to 13,600 tons of rock every twenty-four hours. The cars were pushed into the tipple and turned over, dumping the ore. Since I never worked in the mill or outside on the flumes or dock, I'll leave those details to someone else.

Bob Keating was the shift boss when I began my first day. After about two hours they brought me back to the station to be part of the gang to unload dynamite off the train. Of course, I had lied about working in a coal mine. And, in fact, I had never seen dynamite.

When the boss said, "Join these men and unload the powder train," I wondered why I hadn't asked to work in the mill. Just to mention, the powder was for powder drift loading.

We all took turns picking up a case of powder and carrying it over to the area around the hoist. The big guy in front of me barely leaned over and dropped the case on the ground.

Oh, my gosh! I thought, and I asked him to be a little more careful.

He replied, "You'll get used to it, kid."

And, you know, I did. It wasn't long before I was dropping it just as far as the next guy.

"Why, I hear you can eat the stuff."

"Why, hell! The damned stuff won't hardly go off at all."

Some of those things may be true and I did get careless with it, such as forgetting and packing home a couple of sticks in my back pocket. But, I never did get around to eating the stuff.

A view of central Juneau about the time of these stories. Courtesy of the Alaska State Library, Early Prints of Alaska, PCA 01-527 .

Encounters with the Frenchman

A. J. Mine
Juneau, 1935

HE FRENCHMAN was the Mine Superintendent. He was the boss. The Frenchman was in charge of everything and everybody underground in the A.J. Mine — Alaska Juneau Gold Mining Company. His name was Arthur Reindeau, but everyone called him "The Frenchman." To his face, his old-time friends called him "Art," but we new guys called him "Sir" or "Mr. Reindeau."

Without exception everyone seemed to like him, or at least appreciated the difficulty of his position. Of course, what he said was considered gospel. He was a mining engineer and also served a number of years as a hard-rock miner. His know-how as a real miner stood him in good stead, because he knew the business and wasn't fooled. Along with all of those qualifications, he was alleged to be a good judge of men.

All of us new hires or rehires were first sent to work mucking out the ditch on the main haulage on level number four. I mention rehires because a lot of them were. There were no unpaid vacations and you were never given time off. You were either on the payroll and working or you quit and took time off. The good men were rehired upon their return while the questionable ones were not reemployed.

I saw the Frenchman the first day on the job. While I shoveled the muck — silt that had dropped from the water coming out of ore chute number six — and swung my load across the tracks to deposit the muck for later loading into an ore car, I saw a light advancing up the tunnel swinging back and forth. This struck me as odd because the light was at knee level and most men underground wear their lamps on their heads.

I kept working and when the light came up to me, the man who held it raised it and shined it in my face and said, "What is your name?"

I answered his question and he asked, "You got a cigarette?"

I told him, "No."

He gave a grunt, made a remark that I couldn't hear, and went off up the drift. One of the old-timers came up to me and said, "What did the Frenchman say to you?"

I told him and asked, "Who the hell is he?"

Wow! I thought, when I was told. That's the big gun. I was told that he carried his lamp in his hand swinging up the drifts for two reasons. The first reason was so that he could see better, especially where there was a lot of powder smoke, and, second, so everyone would know that he was coming. He didn't want to find anyone not working. It was pretty obvious that as long as you can see a light, you can tell if a man is working. So you didn't have to be very smart to figure out that the only way to stop working and not get caught was to blow out your own light. But that wasn't so great either, since once your light was out it became 100 percent dark. There was nothing that one could do safely in complete darkness. Also, stopping work meant getting cold. The haulage level was well ventilated and even in the summer, if you didn't keep warm working, you were cold.

The Frenchman stopped daily, asked my name, and tried to bum a cigarette from me. Until my first payday, I was smoking roll-your-owns that I never offered to him. After payday I purchased tailor-made cigarettes and was ready for his daily heist. I cannot remember how many cigarettes I gave him, but there were a heck of a lot. More and more I complained and moaned to myself about the Frenchman not having his own cigarettes. I didn't like it and it really bothered me.

One day, to my surprise, I heard myself say to him, "Mr. Reindeau, I don't think it is right for you to take unfair advantage of your position and bum cigarettes off the hired help. You make more money than I do and I think you should buy your own damned smokes."

"You do, huh?" was his reply. With the light up in my face he said, "What is your name?"

Well, I thought, that takes care of my mining job.

But the boss never fired anyone himself. He always told the shifter to do the dirty work.

At quitting time, I slipped my brass into the wooden dish as quietly as I could but the shifter looked up and said, "Hey, the Frenchman asked about you by name today. What the hell did you do?"

I told him, "Nothing. I just wouldn't give him a cigarette when he bummed me for one."

The shifter said, "Well, hell! He bums everyone for a chew or a smoke. That's the way he does business."

Whew! I needed my job, and it looked like I still had it.

The next day The Frenchman shined his light in my face and said, "I know you're Jeffrey something. Are you going to give me a cigarette today?"

"Nope! I'm not."

The Frenchman came back with, "Well, that's good. I was wondering how long you'd put up with it. I was afraid that you didn't have any backbone."

With that, he took off up the drift swinging his lamp and humming a little tune.

Whew! I thought again.

The next day he shined his light in my face and said, "You're the kid from North Dakota, ain't you?"

"Yes," I agreed.

"Well, hell! How long are you going to muck in this goddamn ditch before you get a better job?"

"You tell me!" I countered. "I sure as hell want something better to do than back and forth with this muck stick." He turned away, grumped and mumbled something that I could not hear. The following day we took up where we had left off.

Much to my surprise he asked me, "How would you like to learn how to be a miner? None of this loading job or bulldozing, but honest-to-god mining?"

Hey! I thought. That would be great!

13

"Well," he said. "You asked for it. It's hard work but, by god, you will make more money and learn something." Up the drift he went.

Wonders of wonders, the next morning the shifter said, "Wait over there." I began mining work as a *nipper* for a mine contractor named Jack Finley. The Frenchman saw me every day when I was on day shift, but never again did he bum me for a cigarette.

I was now a nipper. This was the lowest rank in mining, a real rookie position. But I was happy. Our contract worked three shifts which meant that I had two weeks on swing shift plus two weeks on graveyard shift before I saw daylight again. A nipper is a helper doing everything but running the drilling machines. As a nipper I brought in sharp drill steel and hauled out the dull; prepared the dynamite and primers; helped set up for drilling; and mucked out rock and ran the tugger winch.

We were driving a 5- by 7-foot drift plus pushing up a oreway at a sixty-five-degree slant, so I also mucked out and trammed 18 tons of blasted rock. The other part of my work was operating the tugger winch that lifted men and equipment from number four level at 300 feet up to number three level. I'd take the men and some sharp steel up on the first load so that they could start drilling and I'd lower the skip — or cage — for the remaining gear to go up. I always climbed back up the 300 feet on the ladders and at the end of the shift climbed back down to lower the other two. Doing this gave them maximum time to drill. The sixty-five-degree raise the skip operated in had air and water pipes that afforded our signal line. A short piece of drill steel was used to send the signals. A tap on the pipe from up above meant "all through with the skip" and "you can have it back." A series of bangs on the pipe called me to take the skip up. Two taps on the pipe indicated to lower away with men aboard. Compressed air supplied the power to turn the drum that wound up the wire and raised the skip. The tugger had two handles on it. One handle was the brake and the other was a release that permitted the drum to run free. The rule was to lower the skip with the brake off and it would wind down under compression. It was fast enough with weight in the skip but when the skip was empty, it seemed like it took forever before the skip arrived at the number four level. It was a definite "No!" to release the friction handle. I was told that men have been killed riding down with the friction off because the speed could not be timed well enough and the skip would crash at the bottom. However, it was common to speed up the descent of an empty skip.

On this particular day I ran Jack and Shorty up to the number three level after lunch and shortly got a release—one bell. As usual I released the brake, and the tugger drum started to spool out the cable lowering the skip. I had much to do and just couldn't stand the slow return of the skip, so I released the friction handle.

"Jack the miner" in the snow at the A.J. Mine.

15

Zing! Zing! Whirrl! Whirrl! sounded the drum as it free-wheeled the skip down. Free-falling is the only way to describe the descent. I waited until I estimated that the skip would be about twenty feet above the number four level, just the time to stop its rapid descent. I pulled back on the handle and stopped the spinning drum from maximum to minimum.

Much to my surprise, a hard hat and a lamp crashed down at my feet. I am sure that my mouth dropped open as I wondered what the hell was going on. Then the skip appeared with the Frenchman scrunched down at the bottom. The G-force from the free-fall to almost a full stop must have been tough. In a flash I realized that he had walked down from the number three level from the main shaft and arrived at our skip after it had been released. The Frenchman must have stepped into the skip but didn't have time to signal a man hoist.

With some difficulty, he stood erect and stepped out of the skip. The Frenchman looked at me a long time before he spoke. I could just see him thinking and reviewing the situation. I imagined him thinking how he had stepped into a released skip, knowing that he should have nullified the release signal and then signaled a man hoist. But I wondered if my boss reasoned in the same manner that I did.

The Frenchman looked at me and said, "Son, I've been underground for a long time and I can assure you that the ride that I just had was the fastest ride that I have ever had. I do not recommend it even for my worst enemy. From now on, if you decide to release the friction, I suggest that you walk over and look up the raise to see if there is or isn't a light on in the skip."

With that, he proceeded on his rounds. My job was secured.

I WAS A TEENAGE CHEECHAKO

MY BUDDY, Bill Trumbo, and I were newcomers to Alaska in 1935. I think that we were full-fledged *cheechakos*. From all that I could gather, a cheechako was very much like a tenderfoot or a greenhorn. We qualified. Mountains, forests, glaciers, and salt water were new to us, as were whales, bear, and seals.

We could hardly wait to get out of Juneau and experience the wonders of that beautiful land. As soon as our funds permitted, we purchased an old, beat-up Model-T Ford and headed out the road. We drove north past the duck flats — later to be the airport — for our first view of the Mendenhall Glacier. Awesome! A fork of the road at the head of Auke Bay brought us on Fritz Cove Road that soon ended at water's edge. We didn't know at the time that all roads in southeastern Alaska dead-ended. Some of them were much longer than twenty miles but you still couldn't get there from here.

We were greeted by a black tail-wagger with a throwing stick in his mouth. His owner came out to greet us and said, laughing , "He'll wear you out! Long after you've thrown out your arm, he'll be bugging you."

How true! The Lab was tireless. Later, we borrowed their skiff for our first venture on salt water. Before we had the boat half in the water, the Lab had jumped in. It was a major job to get that darned dog out of the boat. His owners held him until we were about a hundred yards offshore. The moment that they released him, he was in the water following us. They called him back and I'll be darned if he didn't obey.

They yelled to us, "If he does try to follow you later on, don't worry. He's a good swimmer. If he tires, he'll swim home."

Jack and Bill Trumbo driving around the Juneau area.

It was a beautiful day. The water was flat calm and almost high tide. Wooded Douglas Island was over to the west and south. Many seabirds were feeding and flying about. The soaring of an eagle riveted our attention for a long time. Gradually I became aware of a wet, dark head astern of us about a hundred yards.

"Hey, Bill!" I said. "That darned dog is following us."

After checking our position, we were surprised how far offshore we had come. We decided that the best thing to do was to wrestle the dog into the boat. What else could we do? I turned the skiff about and headed back. About twenty-five yards away from him, he raised up for a good look at us and sank down out of sight in the water. We were dumbfounded. For a long time at least it seemed like it there was nothing. His head finally popped up to the left of us about seventy-five yards. That was the first time that we had ever heard of a dog swimming underwater. I rowed toward him and he sank down again. It was then that Bill figured it out.

"That isn't the dog. I'll bet that it's a seal."

Sure enough, it was. Our first wild seal. How dumb can a tenderfoot be?

Our next trip took us out past Auke Bay, Lena Cove, and Tee Harbor to road's end at Eagle River. We turned around and headed back to town. We had seen a single lane, much-used road on the way to the river and decided to take it. It took us to Eagle River Landing.

The Kings were in. A number of boats could be seen trolling back and forth. A dilapidated building served as the fish camp headquarters. A loud, whiskered old guy wearing bib overalls, the operator of the camp, yelled at us, "I ain't got any more good boats to rent, but you can use that water-logged skiff if you can keep it from sinking."

It was a sorry-looking thing and half-full of water. But we took it and he loaned us a hand-line (this was before poles and down-riggers) and sold us some herring.

He told us, "You'd better take two bailing cans 'cause if you lose one you sure as hell will be in deep trouble."

He and his buddies were getting a big kick out of the dry-land farmers going salmon fishing. We were about to cast off when he asked, "If you get a good-sized king, which I doubt, how're you going to land him?"

19

Gosh, I didn't know.

"Well, you'd better take this along, just in case."

With that, he threw what looked like a hay hook into the boat. Well-equipped, we took off.

I'll bet that we weren't out there rowing and bailing more than twenty to thirty minutes before we had a huge strike. I was rowing. Luckily, Bill had a lot of line because that fish took off for Skagway! The line ran through Bill's hands at a rapid rate. As tough as his hands were from pick and shovel work in the mine, the line burned when he tried to slow the fish down. After a while, he could stop the king whenever he made a run. It was then that I noticed that I hadn't been bailing. The water was pouring in at an alarming rate. Bill tied the line to the boat, and helped me bail until the water level was back down to just covering the lower part of our rubber packs. We changed seats and I had the fun of feeling the fish on the line. Soon, I was able to get it up to the boat. The runs got shorter. Bill stood up armed with the gaff hook.

I was yelling instructions, and he was telling me what to do. At the precise moment, Bill swung the gaff like a miner swings his pick. Bingo! He had nailed that salmon right through the body. Not only did the gaff impale the salmon but it also, went right through the planking of the skiff and stuck out a good one and a half inches. The king, at water's edge, thrashed about throwing water everywhere. It was a wild scene! We were yelling. The fish was getting us wet. The boat was filling up with water. We finally calmed down. After bailing enough so that the boat was no longer in danger of sinking, we worked like crazy trying to remove the gaff from the boat. Nothing worked so we rowed back to the landing, and beached the boat so that the left side could not be seen from the building.

The operator and his buddies were drinking beer and swapping lies. I got close to him and in a low voice asked him, "Can I borrow a monkey wrench?"

"What for?" he yelled. "You ain't got a motor. Come on, fellows, let's see what these boys have done."

After all of these years, I can still hear their laughter.

"That's the damnedest thing that I've ever seen" pretty well sums up their remarks. I had to agree.

20

NIPPERS

A. J. MINE
JUNEAU, 1935

M Y EMPLOYER for four years, from 1935 to 1939, was the Alaska Juneau Gold Mining Company. This mine was always referred to as the A.J. At the time it was the largest mine of its kind in the world. This large underground mine employed 650 men working three shifts, plus an additional 350 men working at the huge mill, machine and steel shop, lumber mill, ocean dock, three hydro electric power plants, two tugs, and three barges. The power plants also supplied 90 percent of the power used by the city of Juneau.

I worked underground. At first, I was a mucker — the employee who shovels the muck — rocks, gravel, dirt, and mud. As a rule, what the man actually did on the job was what he was called. For example, there was the shift boss, hoist-man, loader, motorman, powder monkey — dynamite is called powder — pipe fitter, contract miner, and then there were nippers, or helpers.

As I understand it, the designation of a person working in a mine as a *nipper* originated in England and Wales. Prior to child labor laws, it was normal to employ young boys as helpers in the mines. In those days it was quite common to refer to young people as *lads* and *nippers*. It followed that children working in the mines helping the miners were called nippers.

There were many nipper jobs. The steel nipper hauled drill steel. Other specific names for nippers had to do with the products that they transported, such as lumber, powder, and pipe. There was, however, one nipper's job that was very difficult to fill. No, I should rephrase this by saying that it was difficult to keep a man on this particular nipper's job.

The A.J. underground did not have indoor plumbing. The mine did not have wash basins, showers, or flush toilets. Instead, there were honey buckets. The honey buckets were tended by a nipper. This job had been in existence since way back in 1918. As with other nipper jobs, it followed that his job was called the shit nipper.

For quite a while after I went to work underground, I did not know who took care of the honey buckets. One day an old-timer pointed him out to me on the streets of Juneau.

"There he is. That's him over there walking with the lady with a red coat."

How would you like to be walking down Franklin Street with your wife and have people point you out?

"There, right there! That's the shit nipper."

When those men got a few bucks in their jeans and the boss would not transfer them to another job, they quit. It was a problem, and it got worse. Art Riendeau, the mine superintendent, had the following notice posted on the bulletin board at the two stations right alongside the shift boss's office:

NOTICE NOTICE NOTICE

FROM NOW ON, THE JOB OF SHIT NIPPER WILL BE KNOWN AS THE SANITARY ENGINEER. ANYONE REFERRING TO THE JOB OR PERSON AS THE SHIT NIPPER WILL BE DISCHARGED.

I'll tell you, this announcement broke us up. The news of this announcement went through every strata of the Juneau population with the speed of wildfire. It was the announcement of the year.

Nobody got fired. We didn't ever call the man a sanitary engineer. At the same time, the fellows quit pointing him out on the street. The turnover on the job got down to possibly 15 percent.

I Made a Mistake

WHEN I AWAKENED or became conscious, I didn't have the faintest idea where I was. I knew that I wasn't in bed in the Bergman Hotel and I wasn't even sure if I was in Juneau, Alaska. I could hear faint voices of men far away and the hollow sound of footsteps echoing down a hallway. Where was I?

A flood of memories started to come back to me. Five of us fellows had decided to "make a night of it" on the town. It was Friday night. Bill Trumbo and I had Saturday and Sunday off. Working in the gold mine, we had two days off every six weeks which certainly was a good reason to celebrate. Hank Harmon, a manual training teacher at the high school, and two other fellows filled out our group. By midnight the two nameless men had headed home. At 2 A.M. Hank told me, "I give up. I'm going home and if you had any sense, you'd go home, too."

I tried to talk Hank into getting something to eat but he wouldn't go. I had the urge to go home, too, but man I was hungry.

That's what I'll do, I thought. I'll get me something to eat and then go to bed. You see, one of my many problems was that I never get sick or tired like the other guys. All I ever got was hungry.

So I headed down the deserted street to the City Café. The year was 1935. The Alaska Juneau Gold Mining Company was working three full shifts. Halibut fishing employed a number of men with the boats laying over between fishing periods in Juneau. Construction on a number of buildings had a high rate of employment. The result was that a large number of single men were in town.

At the bottom of Franklin Street were the *cribs*, better known as the red-light district. About halfway down the row of houses and across the street was the City Café. My first mistake was that I should have gone home instead of entering the City Café.

It was a slow night for the Café. The counter's twenty stools stood empty. Way back in a booth, three Indians were arguing over some senseless thing.

Gee, I thought, I wish I were in bed. But I'm here so I'll get something to eat. I climbed onto stool number eighteen and waited for someone to take my order. The café was owned and operated by a Chinese family. Charlie took my order and disappeared into the kitchen.

The front door opened and in walked a female alone. Being alone pretty well pegged her as one of the gals from across the street. At my age, nineteen, anyone over forty years of age was extremely old. She not only was old, but not very attractive. To my surprise she walked straight across the room and climbed onto stool number seventeen. After getting herself settled on the stool, she reached over and placed her hand on my thigh and gave me a squeeze. Her makeup was on mighty heavy and she sure smelled of cheap perfume.

I recall these thoughts running through my mind. With all of those empty stools, why didn't she sit elsewhere? Without my asking her, what right did she have to sit beside me, smelling like she did? I was here first, after all. Well, here comes my next mistake. I didn't get up and move to stool number three.

Instead, I heard myself say to my lady of the night, "Hey! I was here first. Why don't you sit someplace else?"

Much to my surprise, she didn't get up and change stools. Instead she yelled to the guys in the kitchen, "Hey, Charlie, this son-of-a-bitch has insulted me."

The waiter came rushing out of the kitchen yelling at the top of his lungs in Chinese. He came around to my side of the counter and grabbed my arm trying to kick me out of the café. After all I was only a one-time customer and the lady was a regular. At the time I felt quite strongly about being unfairly bounced before I had even eaten, plus the fact that I didn't like being manhandled. My very next mistake was to get angry and throw Charlie back to his side of the counter. He yelled to the kitchen help and immediately out came the cook through the swinging doors with a meat cleaver in his right hand. The three Indians, who seemed pretty drunk, lurched out of their chairs anxious to join the fray. At the time I thought, aha, they are going to help Charlie in the hopes of getting a free meal.

In the cowboy movies that I had seen, the hero takes on all comers and wins. In real life, five men, even if three were drunk, is a little too much. I figured that I could stop the first rush and then head for the door. Good old Tom Mix used to equalize the overwhelming odds by grabbing up a chair and using it as a club. Tom Mix-style, I smashed the two Chinese men. Much to my surprise, my chair didn't break up like Tom's. Now, I took a few steps backward to get a good swing at the charging Indians. I hit one of them with a glancing blow and dropped the other two. I recall uttering an odd laugh at the outcome of the fight.

And that was it. That is all I remember about the fight in the City Café.

Now I was back to wondering, "Where am I?"

I started to get scared. My head hurt badly. I couldn't open my eyes. I called out, "Is there anyone here?"

I heard a man's voice close to me. "I was wondering if you were even alive. Where do you *think* you are? You're in jail."

I asked, "What happened?"

"Well, hell," he said, "I don't know what happened. Two cops came into the cell dragging you along the floor. They threw you up on the bunk and took off. I asked them what happened and they told me that it was none of my damn business."

I told my unseen friend, "I can't see anything. Is the light on?"

He came back with, "Of course, you can't see. Your eye sockets are full of what looks like blood and catsup. At least that's what is all over your suit."

He helped me out of the bunk and splashed water in my face until my eyes could open. Wow, did my head hurt!

27

Dayshift came on and they made their rounds. One look at me and the head jailer said, "I think you'd better see a doctor, kid. I'll sign you out and arrange for Dr. Blanton to be at his office."

Before leaving I was told to be at the police court at 10 A.M. on Wednesday. They knew that I couldn't get away because there were no airplanes, ferries, or roads out of Juneau and they always checked every north- and southbound passenger ship.

Dr. Blanton checked me out. My eyes didn't focus correctly. I spent quite a bit of time on the operating table while he cleaned me up. I don't remember how many stitches he told me that it took, but it was around fifty. One thing puzzled the doctor, though: the thick plain glass that he removed from my scalp.

"Oh, of course," he said, "it's from a catsup bottle."

It was then that I remembered my last mistake — I had forgotten about the lady on stool number seventeen. When the Indians pressed their attack, I took a few steps backward directly in her range. She was mad at me. After all, I had insulted her. She grabbed the bottle of catsup off the counter and let me have it. They must have worked me over after I got knocked out because I had black and blue spots all over my body.

I do not recall all of the charges against me, but I think there were at least twelve: destruction of property, assaulting five persons, resisting arrest, among others.

When Dr. Blanton completed sewing me back together, he said, "I have seen the last of the city police mishandling of injured people in the jail. You should have been taken directly to the hospital. You might have died in jail. Besides your other injuries, you had a very bad concussion. I am going to insist that you sue the city."

I showed up at 10 A.M. Wednesday morning. The judge looked at me and said, "I hear that you are going to sue the city. Is that right?"

I stuttered and stammered, thinking, after all, a lone nineteen-year-old boy without any backing had better leave town if he takes on the police.

The judge interrupted my thoughts. "I'll tell you what I'll do. I will drop all charges against you and erase all records of your arrest if you do not sue the city."

It was a good bargain.

I had a date with Ann that Saturday night. I stopped by her place to beg off on the date. One look at me and she thought that I had fallen down a mine shaft.

Two years later another doctor dug some more catsup bottle glass out of my scalp after I did fall down a mine shaft.

The A.J. Gold Mine near Juneau as it looked when I worked there. Courtesy of the Alaska State Library, Early Prints of Alaska, PCA 01-1296.

HERB SMOKED A LOT

A. J. MINE
JUNEAU, 1936

THIS STORY revolves around a cigarette sticking out of Herb's mouth all of the time and our carbide lamps. Prior to the invention of the carbide lamp, miners used candles. Working in that dim, flickering candlelight must have been terribly difficult.

I went to work as a machine man for Herb Knutsen. A machine man does everything the contract miner does, such as drilling, blasting, and timbering. The only exception is that he doesn't know as much nor is his paycheck quite as flush. We were working in a timbered manway and driving an oreway alongside.

Every shift we'd dress in our diggers in the dry room and file past the shift boss's office to pick up our numbered tag. At the end of the shift, we'd return our tag and the shift boss would hang it on its peg. A full board meant we'd all returned. Then we would take our carbide can and fill the lamp with water and carbide. A spin of the wheel on the flint would ignite the gas and we would be ready to strike off on foot to our jobs.

Herb and I never went straight to work upon arriving at the hoist/skip room. Herb always said, "Gotta have a smoke and a cup of coffee before we have at her."

ALASKA JUNEAU GOLD MINING CO.

JUNEAU, ALASKA

P. R. BRADLEY,
PRESIDENT

J. A. WILLIAMS,
GENERAL SUPT.

March 4, 1944

FILE NO. J-33

SUBJECT Personal

To Whom it May Concern:

This is to certify that John William Jeffrey was employed by the Alaska Juneau Gold Mining Company from July 25, 1935 to July 14, 1939.

During all this time he worked underground starting as a laborer and rapidly worked up until he was considered a first class miner.

During the last two years he was employed as a contract miner. His work in this capacity was entirely satisfactory and I recommend him highly for work similar to that he did here.

J.A. Williams

I don't ever remember seeing Herb without a cigarette in his mouth. He smoked all of the time. He coughed a lot, too. While drinking coffee he always took a half-empty package of cigarettes out of his shirt pocket that he had opened before breakfast and replaced it from his lunch pail with a full package. The shirt had two pockets and now they were loaded with forty cigarettes.

"Don't want to run out of smokes," he always explained. After a bit he'd say, "Well, let's have at her," and the skip would rush us up to the landing under the bulkhead for the day's work.

On this particular day we finished drilling and loaded thirty drill holes with 240 sticks of dynamite. The fuses were twelve feet long and burned at the rate of one foot per minute. We cut off the fuses to time the shots, which gave us seven minutes to light all of them, get down to the muck pile, and pass through the difficult opening to the waiting skip below the bulkhead. A good-sized rope was hung down from the bulkhead for us to grab as we slid down from the muck pile. Grasping the rope, we could then swing under the bulkhead to the skip and safety. However, if we missed the rope, we would fall 1,800 feet with no chance of stopping all of the way down.

When all was ready on that particular day, we filled our lamps with a new charge of water and carbide. The flame had to be strong for many reasons, but especially at the blasting face where it got very smoky before the last fuse was lit. Unfortunately, we had trouble lighting some of the fuses because of water leakage out of the face. We had to recut two of the fuses before we could overcome the water-dampened powder in the center of the fuse. Time was running out.

We didn't tarry climbing down the sixty feet of ladder onto the muck pile. As a rule, I was first to sit down on the muck pile for the slide down the incline. Herb always held his light out wide to assist me in seeing the rope. And then with me safe, my light assisted Herb.

Boom! Boom! Boom! The concussion of someone blasting far away came rushing up the dead-end raise. Both of our lights blew out. From habit we both open-handed spun the wheel on our flint, but nothing happened. Then it struck me that our lamps had gotten wet up at the face. Wet flint on steel will not spark. This was a very dangerous situation. It was completely dark. I didn't dare slide down the muck pile in the dark. I would never see the rope. At the same time I didn't dare not take the slide, for within a minute or a little more, the blast would go off and tons of ore would come down on top of us.

All men working underground always carried waterproof match containers.

Herb said to me, "Jack, take off your wet gloves and very carefully dry your hands. I'll dig into my pocket and get out my matches. I will hand you the matches so you can light our lamps. Be sure and don't drop the matches when I give them to you."

It was then that I saw a red glow in the darkness. It was Herb's ever-lit cigarette.

"Stand still, Herb! Don't move!" I said.

I reached over, took his cigarette, and held it to my lamp's gas jet. *Pop!* We had a light! I held my lamp to Herb's, and *Pop!* His was also lit. A hasty slide, a grab on to the rope, and we piled into the skip, and rang many bells to hurry! We were about 200 feet lower when we heard the shots go off.

Wow! That was close! But we made it, thanks to Herb and his ever-present cigarette.

A QUIET TIME

JUNEAU, 1936

I WONDERED, in a typical lifetime, how often does one experience complete silence? In this day and age, we are subjected to a barrage of noise from airplanes, cars, boats, trains, and industry. Then there are the pleasant sounds of a bird's song from a nearby bush, the rustle of leaves moved by a breeze, the call of a quail, and the faint sound of wood being cut far across a northern lake. But complete silence is seldom experienced.

I remember one fall day friends and I went hunting in the Alaskan bush. Juneau, with all of its city noises, was a good forty miles away. There were no airplanes flying overhead. My hunting partners, wherever they were, could not be heard. Even the faint breeze flowing up the grade of this woodland park was slight; it could only be felt on my face. I was experiencing a unique happening, complete and total silence. I checked to be sure that my ears were working by coughing ever so slightly. Everything was so perfect that I even hated to breathe and spoil the moment.

I had been hunting since daybreak. Whenever possible I preferred to hunt alone. After gaining enough altitude, I was side-hill hunting. It is enjoyable to travel at a leisurely pace, stopping often to look and enjoy the scene that develops. I saw a doe with her fawn. A grouse frightened me when it suddenly exploded into the air at my feet. A large brown bear digging skunk cabbage roots on the opposite slope never knew that I had sighted my rifle in behind his right front shoulder and said, "Bang! I gotcha!" I was having a grand time.

The shortage of game had been expected due to the previous winter's deep snow. Unusually heavy snows and an overpopulation of deer made it difficult for animals to get food. Also, as a result of the deep snow, many hundreds of deer drowned. You see, when the tides are out—and Alaska has big tides — the deer go out on to the beaches to eat kelp. Then when the tide comes in again, the deer are often trapped between the high banks and the water.

After a good half-hour of sitting quietly in the sun, I found myself daydreaming. I recalled the time that my friend Hank Harmon and I had gone ashore one morning for a full day's hunt. We climbed through a narrow belt of trees to a large meadow. Hank whispered to me, "Jack! There's a big buck over there on the edge of the meadow."

This photo was taken some time between October, 1935 and May, 1936. On the left is Hank Harmon, in the middle Dick Hall, and I am on the right. Hank was the shop teacher in the Juneau High School, Dick was a loader in the A.J. Gold Mine, and I worked for a contractor at the mine, drilling, blasting and timbering. A remark in our hotel dining room, "Now that is a mean and ugly threesome," prompted Hank to set up this picture. We may not have attained our goal, but it does make a goofy picture.

I whispered back, "You saw him first. He's yours."

Hank raised his rifle and aimed carefully. "Bang!" he whispered. "I'd have gotten him for sure."

"Why didn't you shoot?" I asked.

His reply was, "And spoil an entire day of hunting? Not on your life." I smile to myself as I write this.

I have no idea how long I sat there when I was suddenly aware of movement way down the slope. It was possible to see some movement through the trees. Soon I could see that it was a fine buck deer. The breeze was drifting up the hill toward me, and if I didn't move, he would have no knowledge of my presence. He trotted along at his normal gait, unhurried but with a destination in mind. What a magical sight it was as he moved in and out of the sunlight. I listened for his hoof steps, but the forest floor absorbed all of the sound. He silently passed about twenty-five feet to my right.

Like Hank, I could have shot him — but if I had, I would have forever spoiled the beautiful picture in my mind of the silent woodland and that magnificent buck.

Bill Trumbo, his girlfriend, Jean, and Ann at the beach.

A Rescue

Lena Beach
1936

I
T MUST HAVE BEEN the last of August or the first part of September, 1936. Ann and I were going steady by this time. It was possibly a Saturday when Ann and I and two other couples had a picnic at Lena Beach north of Juneau. The girls were talking while the three of us fellows threw around a football. A pretty stiff breeze was blowing and that is how we first noticed the two middle-aged fishermen.

Two things about the fishermen were different than any we had ever seen. They were in an electrically powered canoe. That was definitely the first and last time that I have ever seen a fisherman after salmon in a canoe. The other difference was that the man in the bow was sitting on a wooden chair. It wasn't a short-legged, modified chair, but a right-out-of-the-kitchen variety. Canoes are unstable enough without raising the center of gravity by siting in a chair. We all agreed those guys were pretty dumb and were asking for trouble. At the time we didn't know how right we were.

About an hour later we heard the most gosh-awful call for help. It was almost a bellow, and then out came "HALP!" "HALP!"

Much to our surprise all we could see were two heads bobbing in the water. The canoe was nowhere to be seen. This was odd. When I took the canoeing merit badge in the Scouts, one of the exercises was to overturn the canoe and have it fill with water. The canoe would not sink. The point of the exercise was to stay with the canoe. We even learned how to get most of the water out of the canoe and climb aboard. Perhaps the weight of the electric outboard, batteries, and the like contributed to the canoe being below the waterline. We were the only people on the beach that we knew of, and so it was up to us to do something.

Obviously we couldn't swim to them. The only means of rescue was to row a boat out to the victims. Down the beach about 300 yards was a huddle of three cabins. Two of the cabins had smoke billowing out of the chimney. We quickly headed that way on the run. The other two fellows, being buddies, stayed together and grabbed the first skiff under the first cabin.

I yelled at them, "You don't have any oars!"

They were much too excited to hear and understand me. Can you believe it? Those two guys launched the boat and jumped in. I didn't notice how they finally got back to the beach. Maybe they paddled back with their hands.

The second cabin didn't have a skiff. The third cabin had an odd-looking thing. It was square at both ends with a little free-board. Actually, it looked a lot like what we used to mix cement in, called a cement boat. The only difference was that this one had holes for oar locks. Again, I couldn't find any oars so I was sure that they were in the cabin.

A lady answered the door. She was Jack Finley's wife. I had worked for Jack as a nipper in the mine. Quickly she showed me where the oars were and I took off. It seemed like only a matter of seconds before I was heading out in my uncertain craft. With the wind blowing and the tide running out, it normally would have been unwise to be out on the water in such an unseaworthy boat. It was less than twelve feet long, and with my weight in the boat, I didn't have over three inches freeboard.

Wow! I thought. How am I going to bring in two men in this thing?

I took one look over my shoulder to make sure I was heading in the correct direction. Thank goodness I was. But I could only see one head bobbing about in the waves. It was then that I noticed that the man left was hanging onto the chair. The chair was keeping him afloat.

Instantly I began reviewing the rules of the lifesaving courses that I had taken through the Red Cross and Boy Scout training. One of the most important rules was that the rescuer must take command of the situation. You must be calm. You must think out how best to make the rescue.

Well, when I got up close to the man, I saw that he was a large, over-weight man. There was no way that I could get him into the boat without shipping a lot of water and maybe even ending up in the water myself. He still yelled pretty loudly and acted sort of wild. So I turned the boat around and rowed slowly toward him stopping still out of his reach.

To this day, I still remember quite clearly what I said to him.

"Mister, this is a very unstable boat. If it wasn't for you, I wouldn't dare to be out here in it. You can't get into the boat. I am going to row you to the beach. Now, I am going to back up to you very slowly. If you make any quick grabs at the boat, and make any effort to climb aboard, I am going to hit you over the head with an oar. Do you understand?"

I got through to him even more than I thought I could. I was surprised how he calmed down. Possibly he thought I was so scared that I might leave him or knock him out if he didn't act wisely.

He came back with, "Look, son, don't get excited. I won't do anything dumb. You back the boat up to me and watch how slowly I will take a hold of the transom."

I backed the boat up close to him and he said, "Look now! I am going to take hold of the boat with one hand. Now, I will take a hold with the other hand. I'm not going to try and get into the boat. I am all right. We will make it fine. Go ahead and row."

Row I did. I had me a great big anchor hanging off the stern. It wasn't long before I realized that I didn't have to row with my left hand due to the wind and the tide. Using both hands on one oar, I rowed and rowed. Oh, but my arms were tired. My anchor kept reassuring me that he was okay and to take it easy and don't wear out. At other times he would moan and say, "Gunnar, why did it have to be you? I'm not good. You are the one who should have been saved."

At long last, I made the beach. My man wasn't all right. He was so cold that he couldn't get up out of the water. The three of us had to wade into the water and carry/drag him up to Finley's cabin. Once we made it to the cabin, we got him out of his water-soaked woolen clothing and into a warm bed. It turned out that he was a local man named Jack Gucker.

I don't recall what happened after that. I suppose that we left him at the cabin and went back to Juneau. The man who drowned was Gunnar Blomgren. Everyone in town agreed with Jack Gucker. It was too bad that Gunnar hadn't been saved instead.

The next night Mr. Gucker came to me and said, "Saying thanks isn't enough. I'd like to buy you a suit of clothes. Don't spare the expense."

And I let him, because he really meant it. It was a nice, dark-brown suit that cost $35. I could have asked for a more expensive suit, but I didn't want to kick a gift horse in the mouth.

About 1962, a fellow came into my office in Seattle. He said, "Mr. Jeffrey, I want to meet you and shake your hand. If you had not saved my dad, I wouldn't be here today. Jack Gucker was my father. I was born one year after the boating accident."

Gunnar Blomgren Is Drowned In Canoe Accident

Juneau Pioneer Suffers Attack, Upsets Craft; Companion Rescued

The body of Gunnar Blomgren, one of Juneau's best-loved citizens, lay quietly last night underneath the gray, tossing waters of Favorite Channel, after an accident stunning in its suddenness and almost fatal to his fishing companion, Jack Gucker.

Strip-fishing from a canoe with a tiny electric motor attached, the two men were plunged into the icy waters when Blomgren stood up, slipped and upset the flimsy craft.

The accident occurred at 3:30 o'clock yesterday afternoon during a temporary lull in the rain that had churned the waters off Louisa Beach into an ugly sea.

Three Juneau young men, Jack Jeffrey, Robert Huntoon and Sherwood Wirt, were playing football on the beach when they heard Gucker's throaty, strangling cries and saw the two men in the water 150 yards offshore.

They sprang quicky to two boats on the beach, belonging to Morris Johnson and Jack Finley, and shoved them into the water. Finding them empty of oars and oarlocks they roused the residents of the two cabins, who had already heard the cries from the canoe.

Jeffrey Makes Rescue

Jeffrey was successful in obtaining the only pair of oarlocks and shot his light rowboat across the waves to the scene of the tragedy, but only Gucker was afloat. He ordered Gucker to cling to the stern of the craft, as the immersed man's bulk prohibited his being hauled aboard.

In a tense race with death, Jeffrey then pulled for the shore, the wind and current, added to his heavy load, slowing his progress alarmingly. Nearly twenty minutes after he fell in, Gucker was dragged out on the beach, more dead than alive, and chilled to the bone.. He was hurried to the Finley cabin, stripped and blanketed and huddled close to the stove, where after two hours he recovered sufficiently to tell the simple details of the tragedy.

Huntoon and Wirt, reaching the upset canoe a few minutes later in a boat without oarlocks, searched in vain for any trace of Blomgren, who had gone under almost without a struggle. Gucker had saved his life by clinging to the canoe chair and a wooden box that had been in the canoe. By the time Jeffrey reached him, he had lost the chair.

Current Strong

Just before the accident, they had shut off the motor and the players on the beach had noticed Gucker paddling vigorously to keep the canoe pointed into the swells, while Blomgren was fishing. They were drifting rapidly northward with the wind and current.

43

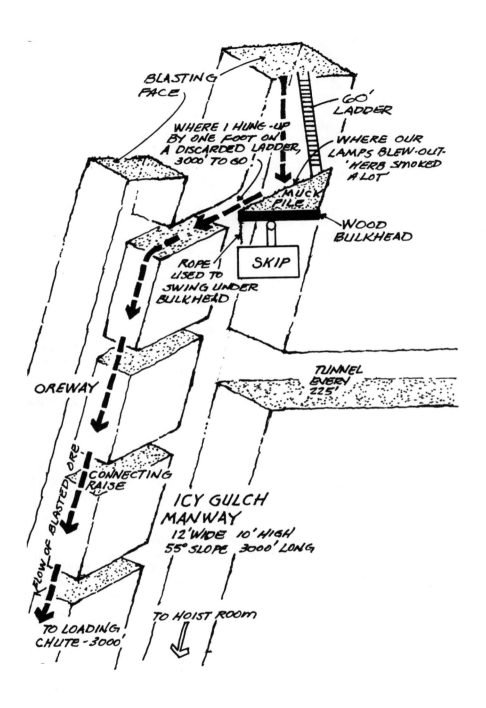

BLASTING
FACE

60'
LADDER

WHERE I HUNG-UP
BY ONE FOOT ON
A DISCARDED LADDER,
3000' TO GO!

WHERE OUR
LAMPS BLEW-OUT-
'HERB SMOKED
A LOT

MUCK
PILE

WOOD
BULKHEAD

SKIP

ROPE
USED TO
SWING UNDER
BULKHEAD

OREWAY

TUNNEL
EVERY
225'

CONNECTING
RAISE

FLOW OF BLASTED ORE

ICY GULCH
MANWAY
12' WIDE 10' HIGH
55° SLOPE 3000' LONG

TO HOIST ROOM

TO LOADING
CHUTE - 3000'

The Icy Gulch mine shaft — how a mine was constructed.

ICY GULCH MANWAY

JUNEAU, 1937

IT WAS 5:30 A.M. on Friday of the last week in April in the year 1937, and I was already running late. After dressing quickly and grabbing my lunch pail on the way out the door, I charged up the trail to the four level of the mine to make the 7 A.M. shift train heading into the mine. If you didn't make the train, you didn't work that day and you weren't paid, either. Being the youngest miner that the A.J. had ever hired, I always felt like I had to work extra hard to prove myself. And I had just gotten a promotion. I was now a contract miner. Maybe they would quit calling me "The Kid."

A number of miners had complained when I was given Herb Knutson's job. I had learned a lot from him. Herb was the contractor and I was his machine man. Everyone at A.J. knew that Herb was one of the best contract miners, bar none. We worked in the Icy Gulch Manway. Icy Gulch was the only hard-rock job in the entire mine that had to be timbered, due to the need of having air and water pipes. It was the manway driven to open that end of the mine. It was timbered, contained air pipes, water lines, track, and a big skip. It was driven at fifty-five degrees, seventy-five feet at a time. An oreway was run up the same height with a connecting raise between. Upon connecting up above, it was barred down and the bulkhead removed. Next came timbering, track, and everything else. Down would go the bulkhead and we would put up another seventy-five feet.

I was asked one time, "How do you get all of your steel, machines, timbers, powder, and everything else from the bulkhead up to where you work?"

The reply was, "You packed it up."

Very often you packed until your knees trembled and you couldn't make the next step on the ladder. Then you would rest long enough to gain strength for the next surge up the ladder. It was tough.

I noticed that Herb coughed a lot and wasn't as strong as I had expected him to be. I soon made a deal with Herb. I would carry all of the heavy loads and see to it that our shift would keep up with the other two shifts. In turn, Herb agreed to teach me a lot of things. Herb was one of those special fellows who knew timbering, pipe work, and mining. And I wanted to learn as much as I could so that I could become a mining contractor myself.

That day came sooner than I had expected when Herb said to me, "Jack, I have decided to pull my plug. I am going to suggest to my cross-shift partners, Ivar and Oscar, to accept you in my place. What do you think? Do you want the job?"

I sure did. And I felt good that, even though I had heard that some were against my promotion, I knew Oscar and Ivar supported me.

As I hunched over to board the shift train that April morning, the engineer rang the electric engine's bell and we took off. The car was lit by a couple of miners' lamps. I didn't as a rule bring my carbide lamp home with me when it was light enough to see coming up or going down the trail on the hill. When I was on afternoon shift, the lamp was handy to light the trail on my downward run.

The three-shift Icy Gulch job was an around-the-clock-operation. We worked seven days before a day off. Starting on Monday, you worked seven days and had the eighth day off. After Friday and seven more days, you had Saturday and Sunday off. Today was Friday and I would soon have two days off. I was looking forward to spending some quality time with Ann. Ann always worried about me in the mine and it was a great relief to her when I had those days off.

Frank Bandy was now my machine man. Frank, no doubt, was

500—4-36

ALASKA JUNEAU GOLD MINING COMPANY

CONTRACT NO. 263

THIS CONTRACT, made and entered into this 23rd day of July, 1938, by and between the ALASKA JUNEAU GOLD MINING COMPANY, a corporation, by L. H. METZGAR, its duly authorized agent, party of the first part and John W. Jeffrey and Vernon E. Hodges,

parties of the second part, all of Juneau, Alaska.

WITNESSETH: That the said parties of the second part agree, at their own expense, to drive Oreway raises in the Perseverance section of the mine, for a contract price of $10.00 per foot; raises to be 7 ft. x 7 ft. in size.

in the Alaska Juneau Gold Mining Company's mine at Juneau, Alaska, on the following terms and conditions, to wit:

First—The work shall be done according to specifications and under the direction of the foreman of the mine.

Second—The parties of the second part shall work on such shifts and as directed by the Mine Superintendent and Foreman

until said work is completed, or until same is stopped by order of the party of the first part, as hereinafter provided.

Third—Said work shall be done in a first class workmanlike manner and to the satisfaction of the foreman of said mine.

Fourth—In consideration of said work, the party of the first part shall pay to the parties of the second part, the contract price above mentioned, as follows:

On the sixteenth day of each calendar month, seventy-five per cent. of the amount earned up to and including the last day of the next preceding month, as per terms of this instrument, which said amount earned shall be determined by deducting from said contract price all costs of labor and material furnished said second parties, by the party of the first part, up to and including the last day of the next preceding month; and the balance at the completion or termination of the whole work under this contract.

Fifth—The party of the first part shall furnish all compressed air necessary to be used in the prosecution of said work, and agree to lend to the parties of the second part all such drilling machines and other tools and appliances as they may reasonably require and request of it in the performance of said work.

Sixth—For the protection of the party of the first part against mechanics' liens, it is mutually agreed that the said party of the first part shall each month out of the moneys due to the parties of the second part, pay the wages of any and all laborers and miners employed on said work by said parties of the second part.

Seventh—Explosives will be furnished to parties of the second part by the party of the first part at the following rates:

Powder $7.50 per case

Primers $0.08 each

Eighth—If any miners and laborers board and room at the boarding and rooming house owned and operated by the ALASKA JUNEAU GOLD MINING COMPANY, said party of the first part, when paying wages as above provided, may deduct the scheduled rate per day in payment of such board and room, and such amount due the Company, is hereby declared a prior claim against any sum that may be due under this contract.

Ninth—The party of the first part reserves the right to put an end to this contract any time the work done thereunder shall fail to conform to the mine workings, as prescribed by the party of the first part or the foreman of said mine, or when the work shall prove unsatisfactory to the party of the first part, or at any other time when the parties of the second part or their employees shall fail to observe the rules and regulations promulgated or enjoined for the safety of the persons employed in said mine or shall fail to exercise the highest degree of care in preventing accident to any person employed in or about said mine.

Tenth—It is further agreed by and between the parties that the party of the first part shall procure hospital services and pay compensation for the benefit of the contractor as well as all men employed by him in connection with the performance of the foregoing contract as though they were employees of the Alaska Juneau Gold Mining Company and it is agreed that the party of the first part may and shall deduct the cost of said hospital services and the estimated cost of compensation monthly from the amount due under this contract.

IN WITNESS WHEREOF, the parties hereto have hereunto set their hands the day and date first above written.

ALASKA JUNEAU GOLD MINING COMPANY,

By _____ Superintendent.

Witnesses:

A. Rendeau

Vernon E. Hodges

My contract with the A.J. Gold Mining Company.

47

CONTRACT STATEMENT
ALASKA JUNEAU GOLD MINING COMPANY

Location of Contract ___160 Stope Perseverance___   No. __234__

162 Lower P.D.	83 @ $ 5.50	$ 456.50		
162 Upper P.D.	82 @ $ 5.50	$ 451.00		
164 Lower P.D.	51 @ $ 5.50	$ 280.50		
164 Upper P.D.	35 @ $ 5.50	$ 192.50		
165 P.D. in Jan.	50 @ $ 5.50	$ 275.00		$ 1655.50

__401__

DEDUCTIONS—LABOR

58	Labor Shifts @ $ 6.10	$ 353.80			
	" " " $	$			
Bonus 58	" " " $ 2.988	$ 173.30			
	" " " $	$			
	" " " $	$			
1 Monkey French "	" " " $	$ 1.15			
	" " " $	$			
	" " " $	$			
Lia. Ins.	" " " $	$ 22.97			
	" " " $	$	$ 551.22		

DEDUCTIONS—EXPLOSIVES

25	Cs. Powder @ $ 7.50	$ 187.50			
600	Primers @ $ .08	$ 48.00			
	Coils Fuse @ $	$			
	Boxes Caps @ $	$	$ 235.50	$ 786.72	

Income per Month and Average per Day $ 14.979 $ 866.78

Less _____ per cent Retained until Completed _____ $ _____

Net to pay this Month _____ $ 865.78

Amount Retained	Contractors	Co. time	Shifts	Rate	Amount
$	Grant P. Logan	4 — 6.60	19	$ 14.979	$ 284.60
$	Jno. W. Jeffrey	2 — 6.60	19	$ "	$ 284.60
$	Everett E. Smith	5 — 6.60	19	$ "	$ 284.60
$	Alex T. Kuporf	4 — 5.65	1	$ "	$ 14.98
$				$	$
$				$	$
$				$	$
$				$	$

INSURANCE STATEMENT

Total Labor Paid _____ (without bonus) $ 353.80

Contractors __58__ Days at __7.10__ per Day for Ins. $ 411.80

Total _____ $ 765.60   @ 3.00 $ 22.97

Cont. No. __234__   Month of __February 1938__

My hours and rates record for the month of February 1938.

aboard in another car. Usually, we were in the same car so that we would have a few short minutes to talk to our outgoing Icy Gulch partners. We always learned important job information from them. This time it was, "We blasted. It sounded like every shot went off."

Off went Oscar and Ivar to a nice, soft bed while we went into the dry room where all of our mining clothing — or diggers — were hung on a big hook. We charged up our lamps and took off after filling the carbide can.

It is the job of the contractor to make the first climb up the ladders after blasting. When the skip arrived under the bulkhead, Frank shouted a "good luck" to me and I secured the short ladder and climbed up on to the bulkhead. The compressed air had been blowing full blast so the air was cleared of powder smoke and there was a slightly cooler feel to the air. The climb up the ladders was a slow, careful trip. Remember, now, tons and tons of big and small pieces of rock had tumbled down this rise a few minutes ago. Big and little pieces of rock would fill up the ladder rungs, or often, the ladder was missing or damaged. One time I found a huge hunk of rock poised on a ladder's holding steel. To explain this more clearly, we hung ladders by drilling holes in the rock where the top rung was. Then we put a piece of broken drilling steel to hang the ladder. Lucky me, I climbed all of the way to the blasting face with little problem. I climbed back down, freeing each rung of the ladders of the many small rock pieces. We had a new seven feet now added to our man-way. Frank and I carried and installed a new very heavy ladder. I went back down to the tool cache for a pry-bar to bar down a few slabs of loose rock. Next, we carried up some staging that we placed on a timber that had withstood the previous blasting.

Frank's lamp wasn't working properly, so he took his lamp apart for a repair job. My light was enough for him to see. It was then that a big slab of rock fell off the hanging wall — which is similar to a ceiling — and turned over the plank that I was standing on. Like being on a spring-board, away I went! I fell straight down, possibly twenty feet before my hard hat and lamp landed and the light went out. In a blink of time my personal lights went out. No pain — absolutely nothing. I was 100 percent knocked-out.

Now, I must tell you what happened according to what Frank later told me. He did not know that I had disappeared from sight. After I fell and my miner's light went out, Frank yelled, "Come on Jack! Turn on your light. I don't think that's very smart."

He flipped on his light to see that I was gone. Then he heard a kind of a moan. He hurriedly climbed down and found me hanging over the draw hole of the ore chute by one foot on the damaged ladder that we had decided could be used. Now Frank had to be careful. It was lucky that he was such a big, strong guy. I do not know how he managed to do this, but he rigged up a makeshift staging underneath me.

Later, he told me, "I wanted to test my footing to be prepared to take your weight." He tentatively touched me and down I came. He saved my life.

I can only guess that he must have dragged me over to the skip, having called the skip to our landing. Somehow he dragged me into the skip and took me down to the four level. By phone they called for a wheeled ambulance and a speedy trip out of the mine—down the tram and to the hospital. I came to en route.

I asked Frank, "How am I doing?"

I remember that he told me the truth, which you're not supposed to do. "I don't know, Jeff. Your nose is torn out from your head. Your head is all cut up and you're bleeding all over the place."

I must have passed out, again.

I became alert on the operating table. I recall asking the nurses not to cut up my clothing because my overalls cost $6 and my underwear cost $4.50. My plea to save money went unheard. During my stay in the hospital I seemed to float between consciousness and unconsciousness. I had no idea at the time whether I had been awake for a minute or an hour. My good friend Hank Harmon came to visit me. I don't remember much of this visit, other than that I was surprised that Hank had gone. Much later Gen, his wife, told me that Hank had come home and said, "I was visiting with Jack, and he must have gotten bored because he just went to sleep. I'm not going to visit him anymore."

This went on and on until I could stay awake for a long period of time. It was then that my doctor had a sit-down visit with me. I mentioned the fact that I could recall moments of being X-rayed or going to or from the X-ray room.

He replied, "Yes, we are considering reporting the number of X-rays done to your head. Possibly this is the most that anyone in the world has had." Then he said, "Do you know, Jack, we have taken some shots of your head to determine the thickness of your skull?"

He handed me an X-ray that showed about two to three inches.

"Your brain is about this big," he added, and showed me an area about as big as a crab apple. Without a smile he got up and left the room.

Hmm, I thought. No wonder I survived that fall.

I do not recall how long I was in the hospital but I couldn't work for four months. The docs did a great job on my nose, returning the base back to my forehead leaving a little scar on the left. The scar on my forehead that reached from my left eye to my hairline protruded so far that I could look up and see it. My head was shaved and exposed many, many cuts all over. I had two black eyes that gradually turned yellowish. My left shoulder had been broken. I was a sight to see.

Three months later, Ann and I got married. Every night she attended to the many cuts on my head and helped me wrap a turban-like bandage around my head. True love this was. Intentionally, we did not have a picture taken at our wedding.

After being on workman's compensation for four months, I returned to work. Much to my surprise, Icy Gulch had been shut down for the entire period of my fall and recuperation. Frank Bandy was now a contract miner. Ivar had retired.

It was an odd feeling to return to the same job and find it just as it was when I had fallen. The dark spot on the rock where I hung from the ladder marked where I dripped until Frank took me down. I never asked why the job was shut down, but I think I know why.

Patsy Ann is still there to greet visitors to Juneau.

PATSY ANN

JUNEAU, 1937

ATSY ANN was a medium- to small-sized, homely dog. Her head and muzzle, plus bowed front legs, harkened back to a bull dog. Her short white hair with black spots suggested a Dalmation may have been way back there in her bloodline. Naw! One thing for sure, her forefathers were not golden retrievers or German shepherds. A longshoreman was heard to say, "Patsy Ann ain't no Lassie or Rin Tin Tin, but she's our mascot. She don't bark and ain't no trouble. She don't dirty up the place."

The place was the I.L.W.U. Longshoremen's Hall that was heated and open twenty-four hours a day. Patsy Ann wasn't any one man's dog, but was a pal to anyone who shared his lunch bucket with her. She lived in the shadows, alleys, and byways until a reporter for the *Juneau Daily Empire* wrote an article about her. The unusual thing about Patsy Ann, he pointed out, was that she met every boat that docked in the Juneau Harbor. Now that is amazing since Juneau had seven docks. She seemed to know in advance at which dock the incoming boat would be tying up. True, the vessels blew their whistle upon rounding the Alaska Juneau rock dump—tailings from the gold mine—but he asked, "How does Patsy Ann unerringly go to the correct dock prior to the arrival of the vessel?"

The Juneau Longshoremen's Union worked the docks as well as dispatching stevedores to work on the ships. Four longshoremen were hired as linesmen at least thirty minutes before the expected arrival of a ship. These are the men who grab the heaving lines thrown ashore by the sailors. The heaving lines are attached to the vessel's hawsers that are then hauled ashore and placed on the dock cleats. This enables the ship to be secured alongside the dock.

The arrival of any vessel was an occasion — sometimes, almost carnival-like. As a rule, the open dock face was filled to capacity with local people prior to the gangplank being set in place. A number of these people might be there to meet a member of the family or a friend returning from the "outside." At that time, Alaska was still a territory. Others were there to meet friends en route to their homes further north. Possibly, half of all those present were there just for the hell of it. What about Patsy Ann?

As I walked toward the dock around 8:30 one morning, I suddenly knew that I had the answer to the "mystery." The *S.S. North Sea* was due at 9:00 A.M. The Northland dock was on lower Franklin Street across from the red-light district and just past the longshore hall. I set out walking at a fast pace as it was necessary that I be on the dock prior to 8:30. I walked into the warehouse about 8:20 and the *North Sea* was not yet in sight. Orrin Kimball, the assistant agent, told me that the ship would be about fifteen minutes late. A few minutes later, four union linesmen strolled into the warehouse and entered the lunchroom. Lagging behind the men was slowpoke Patsy Ann. She was not allowed in the lunchroom, so she proceeded on through the warehouse out on to the open face of the dock. She stood sentinel there for over half an hour before people started to arrive and the linesmen came out of the lunchroom to retrieve the heaving lines that the sailors threw ashore.

There was an obvious answer to the reporter's question. As well, a number of people familiar with the shipping business knew the answer, but joined in a conspiracy of gleeful silence. It was also quite possible that the reporter got a kick out of conning his gullible public. I joined in telling only Ann, my wife.

Now after fifty-eight years, the truth is out. Patsy Ann did not unerringly go to the correct dock prior to the arrival of the vessel. She merely followed the dispatched linesmen. This was nothing new. She had been following linesmen to the various docks for years!

The statue of Patsy Ann greets ships arriving in Juneau, much as the real Patsy Ann once did.

There's a new answer to the mystery of Patsy Ann, the town dog who became famous for meeting every ship during the 1930s.

Though deaf since puppyhood, she somehow knew when ships were coming and at which of Juneau's seven docks they'd tie up.

Patsy Ann's ability to meet every boat took on the status of legend. In 1934 the mayor dubbed her "Official Greeter of Juneau, Alaska" and exempted her from a licensing law. Tourists took her photo, shops sold Patsy Ann postcards and the newspaper reported her adventures.

For years people theorized and joked about how Patsy Ann knew where and when to meet the boats. Could she feel the ships coming, the way dogs are believed to sense earthquakes? Did she have some kind of canine premonition? "Most boats had a regular schedule and I know they were posted in the paper," said city museum curator Mary Pat Wyatt. "Maybe she read the paper?"

More likely Patsy Ann followed the longshoremen down to the docks, said Jack Jeffrey, who lived in Juneau in the 1930s. He did a little sleuthing one day in 1937 to test his theory.

Jeffrey, who now lives in Green Valley, Ariz., was waiting at the longshoremen's hall when four linesmen strolled into the warehouse, followed by Patsy Ann. She took up her post on the dock while they waited inside the lunchroom.

"The linesmen, they were there ahead of time, but they were always sitting out of the weather," Jeffrey said. "But Patsy Ann, she had to be out on the dock."

The record verifies Patsy Ann chose the longshoremen's hall as her home. She died there in 1942.

Seven years ago a memorial statue of Patsy Ann was erected. The Gastineau Humane Society gets letters from people all over the world who have visited the statue and want to know more, said Director Linda Blefgen.

"People just walk by and pat her on the nose," Blefgen said. "They are drawn to her story."

Children's author Beverly Woods was haunted by Patsy Ann after she heard the story.

Patsy Ann became the main character in Woods' book, "Dogstar," in which a 13-year-old visits contemporary Juneau on a cruise ship. He encounters Patsy Ann in an alley, and she takes him back to her time — 1932.

A percent of profits from the book go to a non-profit group working to pay off the downtown Juneau sculpture of the dog.

Jack Jeffrey's theory may be true, said Woods, but it's not as satisfying as the legend.

"I prefer to believe that she sensed something that humans could not see or feel," Woods said. ◆

A recent local newspaper account of Patsy Ann.

Jack and Ann at the Mendenhall Glacier.

ICE SKATING

THE MENDENHALL GLACIER, 1937

I REALLY LIKE this photo of Ann and me ice-skating on the lake in front of the Mendenhall Glacier. In fact, I wish that we had photos of the many, many outdoor activities we enjoyed together. We ice-skated, snow-skied, climbed mountains, fished, swam, boated, water-skied, and roller-skated. Often we hunted deer, caribou and moose, tented, trailered, and traveled overseas to Europe and Down Under. However, there was one thing that Ann would not do. She refused to go mountain goat hunting, saying that it was just too dangerous. She would tell me, "If you and your nutty friends want to do it, go! But leave me out!"

As a rule, we lost about three goat hunters a year on the Kenai Peninsula, either in an airplane accident or falling off a cliff. After I spent one, long, cold night stuck on a ledge — a small stream of water froze just two feet from where I was trying to sleep — I knocked off mountain goat hunting.

But back to the Mendenhall picture. At the time the photo was taken, we were fortunate not to have snow. As you no doubt know, a beautiful snowfall of just two inches is curtains for ice-skating. We could hardly believe it! The word was out! The lake is frozen! No snow! You'd better get out there before the snow comes!

And we did. The girls whipped up a picnic lunch and we headed out the fourteen miles to the glacier. The Parks Department had a picnic area with benches and tables, plus a roofed area in case of rain. I don't recall how big a party we had, but I do know that my buddy Bill Trumbo and his girlfriend, Jean, were present and took the picture.

The glacier had a vertical face right down to the frozen lake and it was fun standing there on the ice with our hands touching the glacier as high as we could reach. Ann recalls the ice cracking loudly, at which we beat a hasty retreat. It was 1997 when we last saw Mendenhall and were amazed at how far it has retreated. I wonder how many people have had the opportunity to skate right up to a glacier's face?

PETERSBURG

ETERSBURG is a small fishing town 120 miles south of Juneau on Mitkof Island. You don't have to be of Norwegian descent, but it helps! Before World War II, Petersburg was the richest town per family in Alaska. Seine boats, trolling boats, halibut schooners, and shrimp boats brought in the funds for the villagers. Most of these boats were quite high-tech and expensive.

I was sent to Petersburg in June 1939 to learn the business of a Wildlife Agent for the Federal Alaska Game Commission. My home was *the M.V. Black Bear* where I also was the chief cook and bottle-washer. This was the first time I'd been away from home since Ann and I were married and found it very lonesome with little to do other than work, cook, do dishes, and attend the local movie house.

The Game Commission boats, as well as the fishing fleet, had recently installed radiophones. They were new and not as sophisticated as the sets are now. I believe most villages didn't have their electrical systems grounded and other factors must have come into play to make it possible for the happening in the theater this day.

I went to the early movie. Midway through the show, when the hero had his fair maiden in his arms and he was telling her "My dear, I love you with…," a loud and clear Scandinavian voice drowned out our hero's voice.

"Calling the *Thora J.* Calling the *Thora J.* Are you dar, Lars?"

"Yah, I'm here. Back to the *Wanderer,* over."

"Yah, how is fishing over dar? It's no good har, over."

"It's pretty good. Why don't you fish here? Over."

"Yah, sure, ver are you? Over."

"Wal, remember where Ole fell overboard? That's where we are."

Our movie hero then interjected, " …Will you be mine?"

Nobody but me seemed to be surprised at the interruption. Our hero did marry the girl. We all hoped the *Wanderer* had good fishing!

Jack and George Gullifson standing midship on the M.V. Bear.

The Black Bear *coming into dock at Petersburg.*

The Black Bear *docked at Petersburg.*

Above: Jack on the stern of the Black Bear; *Bottom: The* Black Bear *on the grid.*

HOSEA SARBER

KETCHIKAN, 1939

I T WAS IN JULY 1939 that I was accepted a position to work as a special agent for the Alaska Game Commission. They kept me around the headquarter's office in Juneau for a few weeks and then sent me to Petersburg to work with their best wildlife agent, Hosea Sarber.

They gave me a pretty good rundown on Hosea. He was in his early forties, married, with one small child. Prior to going to work for the Game Commission, he had been a game guide specializing in Alaska brown bear hunts. In fact, he was considered one of the two foremost experts on brown bear in the world. They mentioned, in passing, that he was blind in his left eye. Despite this handicap, his one-eyed vision was 20/20, and he was an expert with a rifle, handgun, and shotgun. I was told that I would learn many things from Hosea during this breaking-in period.

The Game Commission had their own float in the small boat harbor in Petersburg. We tied up across the float from the *M. V. Black Bear*. All along, I had wondered where I was to be quartered. The *Black Bear* was my home, I soon learned. Howard Jensen, a former halibut fisherman, was the skipper of the 38- foot *Black Bear*. He welcomed me aboard and showed me my bunk and the galley. It was then I learned that I was to be the cook and deckhand. Considering my lack of expertise or

Hosea worked off a big boat and patrolled the rivers and bays in an outboard-powered speedboat. In those days the outboards did not have a gearshift and were always started in gear. Well, Hosea went alone for a day's patrol and did not return. His speedboat was found run hard-up on the beach with the tank empty. The best guess about what happened was that he had trouble starting the motor and stood up to give some good pulls on the starter rope. The motor must have suddenly started up and thrown him out over the stern. He was wearing heavy clothing and hip boots, and swimming in that cold water for any length of time was unlikely. His body was never found.

experience in the kitchen, you can imagine the meals that I put out — or more accurately, didn't put out!

After exchanging sea stories over a cup of coffee with Howard, the *M. V. Bear* took off for Ketchikan. Howard and I walked the long dock approach to the beach in town and one block to the upstairs office of the commission.

At the foot of the stairs, Howard said, "I'll not go up with you. I think that it would be best if you had your first talk with Hosea by yourself."

I thought that this was a little odd, in fact, strange, but that is the way it was to be.

The door was open and in I walked. My immediate attention was directed to a large photo of Hitler on the far wall. As you can imagine, Hitler was a dirty word. It is difficult to explain my reaction. I was outraged. Imagine a Nazi sympathizer right there in a United States Government office. Oh, yes, there were rumors about German people being situated at strategic entrances to bays in southeastern Alaska, people who had been planted there years ago. But planted in this little government office, it didn't seem possible. Our conversation wasn't very spirited. My immediate plan was to be transferred to another station as soon as possible. My thoughts were jarred when Hosea looked at the clock, and opened the right-hand drawer of his desk. To my amazement, he pulled out a .38 revolver and checked the cylinder for shells and said, "Every hour on the hour, I have target practice, dry-shooting, of course."

With that, he aimed at Hitler and fired off six quick shots. My mouth must have dropped open and the confused expression on my face prompted Hosea to explain.

"My folks came from Germany. I speak the language quite well. My relatives in the old country have written from time to time about what is happening to Germany. They don't like it and I don't like it. That is why I dry-shoot the S. O. B. every hour on the hour."

He went on to explain that he believed Hitler should be killed before he led Germany into the next world war.

"In fact," he said, "I wrote to the government and volunteered to go to Germany and kill Hitler."

65

I suggested that he was joking and wondered out loud how he thought that he could get away with it.

While in his early twenties, he had sailed in the merchant marine from the East Coast to Europe, including Germany.

"If you want to smuggle anything into a country, the easiest way is as a sailor on a cargo ship. Once you are checked out and cleared, you come and go. I could easily get a knocked-down rifle ashore and hide with my relatives. Speaking the language and dressing the way that they do, I would be accepted. I can shoot accurately up to 800 yards with a scope. I have no doubt at all that I can kill that bastard and get away." He said that he would have no qualms about shooting Hitler, since he was a mad dog.

By now I was on the edge of my chair, and asked, "What was the government's reply?"

The reply was to the effect that they would have no part in an assassination, despite the obvious good it would do for the world.

I was impressed. Looking at him, I believed that he could have done it. What a change in the course of history there would have been if Hosea had been given the go-ahead.

A BLUE FOX SKIN

JUNEAU, 1939

M AGGIE CAME ACROSS the hall to my office and said, "Jeff, the boss wants to see you."

I looked at my watch. It was a few minutes after 9 A.M. "Have you any idea what he wants?" I asked.

She shrugged her shoulders. "All I know is that he had a telephone call and then asked me to give you a yell."

Frank Dufresne, the executive officer of the Alaska Game Commission in Juneau, had a big grin on his face when I stepped into his office.

"Jeff, have you ever been down at the 'line'?" He was referring to the red-light district situated at the lower end of Franklin Street.

I laughed and said, "Oh, sure, I go down there whenever my wife will let me."

"Seriously," he said. "I have a little job for you and it most likely involves you arresting one of the whores."

He explained the situation to me. It seemed that Mr. Gotstein, a fur buyer, had called him that morning advising that he had in his possession an illegal blue fox skin. One of the gals from the line had come to see him the day before offering to sell an unsealed blue fox skin.

"As you know, Jeff, every blue fox farmer is issued his individual seal that identifies the owner of the skin, thus preventing thefts. I want you to go see Mr. Gotstein and take it from there."

As directed, I went to see Mr. Gotstein and he told me that Helen Anderson had come to him with an unsealed blue fox skin. He guessed that she was a prostitute and asked her if she had taken it as a trade. Mr. Gotstein explained to her that it was an illegal pelt and that he would have to seize it and turn it over to the Game Commission. Luckily, he had asked for her address, which was 216 South Franklin Street. I signed for the pelt and left.

The very first thing that I did was to call my wife, Ann, at her office. I certainly didn't want someone telling Ann that her husband had been seen entering one of the houses on lower Franklin. I told her that I had official business to attend to and that I'd tell her all about it at lunchtime.

I parked the commission car on the street in front of the house and rang the doorbell a couple of times before the madam opened the door. She greeted, "It's kind of early, young man, but come in."

I told her that I was on official business and needed to talk to Helen Anderson. She seated me in the parlour and went to find Helen. Most likely she was still in bed, because it was a long time before she appeared. Apparently, she hadn't been told that it wasn't a customer waiting to see her, because she was all prettied up and wore a very thin, see-through dressing gown. Helen was a nice-looking woman — and I could see all of her — of about twenty-five years of age.

I told her, "Hold it right there! I am not a customer! I'm a Federal Game Commission Agent and I am here to talk to you about the blue fox skin that you tried to sell to Mr. Gotstein. I must ask you to go back to your room and put on some clothes."

I smiled at her and continued, "If you don't cover yourself up, I won't be able to keep my mind on what I am here to do."

When she returned, she was completely straightforward about how she acquired the skin.

Helen told me, "Olaf Larson came to me with the fox skin. He didn't have any money but, gave me the fox skin for a piece of tail. So I turned a trick with him, thinking the fox skin must be worth more than my standard charge for a 'quick lay.' " Remember, those were her words, not mine.

Helen didn't know where Olaf lived but seemed sure that the bar next to the City Café would know.

Helen was a pretty, soft-spoken lady. I think I had expected a floozy with wild hair, a cigarette in one hand, and a drink in the other. No. Instead, she could have been accepted into any home in Juneau. I had a strong urge to go into my missionary mode and ask her what a lovely girl like she was doing in a place like this.

I did find Olaf. His room was a dark, smelly, rat's nest of a place. He was still in bed, sleeping it off. It looked like he had slept in his dirty long johns for at least two months. He was dirty, unshaven, and in general a horrid person. I was happy to arrest him and haul him off to jail. To this day, I can't understand how Helen could have stood being near Olaf, let alone take him to bed.

HOSEA'S BEAR HAT

ADMIRALTY ISLAND, 1939

I AWAKENED with a start. The dream was as vivid and scary as the real-life experience had been back in 1939. A huge brown bear was charging us. In a calm voice, Hosea said to me, "Don't shoot."

Hosea Sarber was the senior Wildlife Agent for the Federal Alaska Game Commission. He was my mentor, as I was the newest hire with the commission. We had motored over to Pybus Bay on Admiralty Island from Petersburg the night before on the *M. V. Black Bear* in the company of Howard Johnson, skipper, and Malcolm Greaney, a professional photographer. We were expected to protect Greaney as he recorded brown bear catching salmon in their natural habitat.

We had discussed brown bear at breakfast and Hosea had said, "Most of the time, a charge by a bear can be avoided, especially if it starts out as a bluff. However if you shoot, the charge will continue. Then you just hope you can get off enough shots in a short time to stop him."

His voice turned very serious when he told me, "The Juneau office sent me your file. I was impressed with your qualifying twice for expert rifleman and your shooting on two championship rifle teams. They even included a clipping from the *Daily Alaska Empire* telling how you had saved Jack Gucker from drowning. Now, I must ask, when the chips are down, do you believe you can hang in there?"

"Well," I said, "in other tight situations I have done okay. But afterward, the jitters and shakes set in."

He replied, "Well, sure!" In relief, he slapped my shoulder and said, "Okay, let's go."

Prior to our leaving on the boat, Hosea said, "I must remember to take my 'Bear Hat.'"

Actually, it was an old-fashioned military campaign hat, similar to those worn in the National Guard during the early '30s, and it was pretty beat-up looking. I indicated as much.

Alaskan bear fishing in a stream, just as Hosea found his.

Hosea said, "Yep, it has lots of old deer smells, goats, sheep, beaver, and moose smells. It's a powerful smelling hat where bears are concerned."

Hmm. I wondered what he meant.

Because of a high wind and poor anchorage, Howard stayed behind with the *Black Bear* while Hosea, Malcolm, and I took off in the skiff at dawn. Hosea was armed with a "big-bear gun" and I had my trusty 30-0-6. Malcolm was loaded down with many still and motion cameras, and since this was the age of light meters, he had those to carry as well. He got some great shots of bear fishing with no problems. The ones fishing downstream would usually sense our presence and go into the woods, only to reappear way downriver from us. When we saw a mother bear with two cubs heading our way, we disappeared into the woods until she was far below us. Like Hosea said, "We don't want to mess around with that old girl."

But then, here came an old bear acting like he owned the stream we were on. He quit fishing after spotting us and started to roll his head from side to side and made threatening short rushes at us. Hosea talked to him all of the time in a conversational tone.

"Now, look here, Mr. Bear. I don't think that you want to give us any trouble."

And to us, "Be sure and don't turn and run. We will slowly back up so as to give him some room. We want to keep out of his space, because that is when he will feel pressured to do something."

Hosea kept talking to reassure the bear, and also me. But, hey, the bear kept coming as we backed up.

Hosea said, "The way that this bear is acting, I might have to take extreme steps to stop him."

I assumed that this meant shooting the bear. I already had a cartridge in the barrel and the safety off. Wow! Here he came!

That's when Hosea said, "Don't shoot! "

Quick as a flash, he grabbed his bear hat and sailed it like a frisbee at the bear. The bear grabbed it, bit it, tore it, and stomped on it. In the meantime, the three of us backed up into the woods and made like ghosts into the timber.

By this time, I was shaking all over.

Hosea said, calm as could be, "Doggone it! That's the third bear hat I've lost. Just when I get it smelling just right and fitting my square head, some mean old bear chews it up. But then, I'd rather it was my hat than my leg."

THE BALD EAGLE

I DOUBT if I had a sighting of one eagle until 1936 because of the comparatively few eagles that were left. The territory of Alaska paid a bounty on eagles, as well as on wolves and seals. Besides the bounty, eagles were being killed in large numbers for their feathers to be used for ceremonial purposes. DDT and other poisons were beginning to be used. Even lead from hunters' shotguns settling on the shallow bottoms of sloughs and lakes got to the eagles, via ducks eating the pellets, and then the eagles eating the ducks. Yes, the bald eagle was headed toward extinction.

During this same time, every reference book that you picked up referred to the eagle as a "bird of prey." Predators are not protected and most often there is a bounty paid to hasten their demise. Back then in the States, ranchers and farmers hated the eagle, claiming that they lost many of their calves and lambs to eagle kills. Farmers and hunters claimed that the eagles were killing useful game, such as ducks, rabbits, pheasant, and other species that people eat. In Alaska, the canned salmon industry and fishermen were the strongest advocates for the bounty on eagles. When I heard how the fishing industry lobbied the delegates and passed money freely to both the Republicans and Democrats, I understood how, eagerly, these bounties were sanctioned.

I was employed by the Alaska Game Commission in 1939 as a special agent. My area consisted of the northern section of Southeast Alaska, taking in Juneau, Sitka, Haines, Skagway, and the small native villages like Hoonah, Angoon, and Pelican City. In the early fall of 1939, our boss, Frank Dufresne, received a directive from the parent organization, The Biological Survey in Washington, D.C., to place into effect an immediate survey to last one year to determine if bald eagles really were predators or basically scavengers. At the time, there were only ten field agents in all of Alaska. This directive only affected five areas in Alaska where eagles live the year round, namely Ketchikan, Petersburg, and Juneau in southeast Alaska and Cordova and the Kenai Peninsula to the west. We were instructed to take, if possible, at least one eagle a month for twelve months. The contents of the stomach were to be placed in a wide-mouth mason jar, and the jar filled with formaldehyde. When a carton of jars was complete, we were to send the carton to a lab in Denver. The lab would examine the contents of our yearly survey and determine if the bald eagle was a predator or a scavenger.

We hated the idea of killing so many of the already depleted species, but we were assured that this was the only way to go. We were issued 220 Swift rifles equipped with scopes, plus mason jars and jugs of formaldehyde, so we could kill eagles in order to save them. Believe me, it wasn't easy. Seldom could I see an eagle perched on a high tree from ashore. Shooting from a boat, except in calm weather, was a challenge. We always waited until about 10 A.M., since eagles only hunt during the daylight hours and we wanted their stomach full. Once we had an eagle down, we slit open its throat where we could feel a large lump below the beak and above the body. We tied off the top entrance with twisted rubber bands and then the bottom of the stomach. Surprisingly, sometimes the stomach content was so large that I had to milk it into the jar. Hosea Sarber, an experienced agent, was better at this than most of us and he produced more jars in the year than anyone else.

I remember the time that we were on patrol down Chatham Straits, not far from the native village of Angoon, when I had an unusual taking of an eagle. The *M. V. Bear* was used as the home base, but most of the patrolling was done on our 16-foot speedboat. Speed is relative to the date and equipment available. We were booming along in our decked-over-bow boat powered with a 25-horse Evinrude. We sighted an eagle high up on a cedar tree, so we went ashore. The 20-foot tide was out with a lot of beach exposed on this small island. Yes, I could see the bird so I took careful aim and down he came. I found him at the bottom of the tree. He was scary to see. Birds can puff themselves up to look oversized and he was in a fighting stance — an aggressive stance, I must say. I had winged him unfortunately, and he was ready to fight. Hissing and hopping toward me, he presented himself in a very threatening manner. Alas, I had to dispatch him with my pistol. His stomach didn't leave much room in the jar for formaldehyde.

As a result of our study, bald eagles in Alaska were determined to be basically scavengers. The study was turned over to the U.S. Senate and House. The Bald Eagle Law was passed in 1940 for the lower forty-eight states, but Alaska was not included because it was still a territory. The powers that be kept after Congress until Alaska was included in this law in 1952. Apparently, there were holes in the 1952 bill, so it was tried again in 1972. This time the protection of the bald eagle became law. It was a long struggle, but well worth it. This is one operation that I was very proud to have participated in.

SUBPOENA JONES

T**O MY KNOWLEDGE** this story has never been written down other than in the transcripts of the federal court in Juneau. However, hundreds of Alaskans have read the court's records and the story has been recounted many times. The tale, with its punch line, could be told on less than one page. However, if one did not live in Southeastern Alaska during the early 1930s, it might be difficult to understand how this story could be true. Therefore, I will start at the beginning and tell you how it was back there in 1932.

But first, I will tell you how I learned that the story was true. One day while on a Game Commission river patrol up the Taku River, we came upon a hunter's camp. One of the hunters was Federal Judge Folta. Of course, I knew who he was, but being on a lower strata in the scheme of things in Juneau, I doubt if we would have ever been friends had we not met in the camp.

Weeks later we met again in the hall of the federal building. Making small talk, he asked me where I'd been of late. I told him I had just returned from patrol in the icy straits area including Hoonah.

"Hoonah!" the Judge said. "Have you met my friend Marshal Jones?"

I told the Judge that I knew the marshal.

"Good," he said, "then you must read the court's records of the time that he brought a native girl and other witnesses to the court in Juneau from Hoonah on the *M. V. Estebeth*."

He took me into the records room and there opened on a small desk was the transcript of the court proceedings. The pages were smudged, indicating that it had been read and handled many times. After all of these years, I cannot recall exactly what I read word for word, but I'll fill in the best that I can.

The background to the story begins with the *M. V. Estebeth*. Everything and everybody in Southeastern Alaska moved from place to place by boat. Oh sure, float planes were flying and moving a few people who could afford the trip, but 99 percent of the people rode on boats. One may ask, "Why didn't they travel by roads?" All cities, villages, canneries, and logging camps in Southeastern Alaska are on islands with the exception of Juneau, Haines, and Skagway. One can't count Haines or Skagway because they are way up Lynn Canal and should be part of the Yukon Territory. Juneau is landlocked by glaciers and mountains. Every five years the United States Post Office let out bids for the service of carrying the U.S. mail to these isolated villages, canneries, camps, and dogholes, as they were called. Those bidding were required to have a vessel capable of not only delivering the mail, but providing passenger service and carrying cargo billed to these out-ports. The owners and operators of the *M. V. Estebeth* repeatedly won the Juneau service bid from the 1920s through the 1930s. It was just under 100 feet and averaged twelve knots with a crew of six men. They ran night and day in good weather or foul. Good weather found them in their homeport for two days a week. In January and February they often limped into Juneau the morning of the eighth day, heavy with ice.

One of the Indian villages they served was Hoonah. I recall seeing a few white people at the time in town such as schoolteachers and a store keeper. Deputy Marshal Jones was one of the white people. He was in his forties and unmarried. He had quarters behind the two-cell jail. I noticed and was told that he had from one to three native girls keeping house for him and doing the cooking. Nobody knew the arrangements he had with the girls. It was rumored that since the girls' homes were not the best, that he let them stay at his place if they kept his house up and satisfied him.

Now, we need to go into the judicial system of Southeastern Alaska. Court was held in Juneau about every three months. During the periods between court, there would be unlawful acts committed. As a rule, those responsible were arrested and released pending court time. The real violent criminals were put in jail. Prior to court time, Marshal Jones would round up his people and bring them on the *Estebeth* to Juneau.

At the time of our story, George Folta was the district attorney. He explained and reminded me that in 1932, the older natives did not speak English. The schools taught English. The amount of English that the younger native people knew depended on the amount of schooling and practice. As a rule, their vocabulary was limited. That was the problem our heroine, Annie Johnson, had when she was called as a witness.

"Calling Annie Johnson to the witness stand." Someone nudged her no doubt, and she slowly walked up to the front of the court.

"Raise your right hand and state your name."

Expecting some trickery or possibly an embarrassing situation created by the white man, she said, "You know my name."

It was explained that in a court of law one must answer all questions regardless of the number of times they are asked. Annie Johnson was instructed in other responsibilities of being a witness but was most of all told that the most important thing to remember was to tell the truth.

"Where do you live?"

She replied, "Hoonah."

"Do you know the defendant?"

"No."

I will rephrase the question. "Do you know Milo Minok?"

"Yes."

There were other questions establishing the fact that she was a reliable witness.

"Were you subpoenaed by Marshal Jones?"

"Yes. Once in Hoonah and twice on the *Estebeth*."

It was very difficult for the judge to maintain order in his courtroom since he was rolling in the aisle himself.

From that day forward, Marshal Jones was called Subpoena Jones.

A Day On Patrol

"OKAY, Jeffrey! Go ahead and do your stuff. Chart the course down Seymour Canal while we raise the anchor."

Don Gallagher, the skipper of the Alaska Game Commission boat the *M.V. Bear* said the commission had two other boats patrolling southeast Alaska. The *Grizzly Bear* was stationed in Ketchikan and the *Black Bear* in Petersburg. I first crewed on the *Black Bear*, skippered by Howard Jensen. Howard spent hours schooling me on navigation and general shipboard activities. Hosea Sarber, the wildlife agent, in turn drummed into me Alaska game laws and how to proceed as an agent. I *graduated* and took over the duties of a special agent, covering the Juneau/Sitka area patrolled by the *Bear*. The year was 1939.

We had returned from an early morning hike into the Pack Creek Reserve, set aside for the large Alaska brown bear. The area is on Admiralty Island, south of Juneau and up at the head of a long arm of water named Seymour Canal. As usual in Southeastern Alaska, lacking roads, bridges, and ferries you can't get there except by boat or float plane. The salmon run was in full swing with the fish returning to spawn. Our mission was to check out the stream, count the number of bear we saw fishing, and determine whether or not the bear population and the salmon migration were normal.

Some years back, a 17-foot-high viewing platform had been erected on the south fringe of the timber, opposite the mouth of the creek. From that height and aided by glasses, we could see a good distance up the stream. On average, six to eight bears could be seen at one time, with more showing up around the first bend of the river. I was surprised to learn that the bears only fished heading downstream. But that made sense, as you will soon discover.

It was interesting how the bears had learned to accommodate one another, some fishing fast and others slow. When a faster bear would overtake a slower, smaller bear, the latter would simply go off into the woods. Obviously, there would be constant confrontations if the bears were fishing both up and down a stream. A well-worn path into the woods was used by all for returning upstream. There was an exception to the rule. Mother bears with a cub or two were given a wide berth. The rule in the wild is, "Don't mess with a she-bear and her cubs. Humans must never get between a mother bear and her cubs. There would be an almost certain, fatal outcome.

To our delight, a mother with two cubs came into view around the bend. Of course, she had the right of way. Big or small, the other brownies gave her a wide berth. She proceeded downstream at her own pace catching salmon with the three of them eating their fill. It was with interest that we observed them up close at the mouth of the stream. It became obvious that she had decided it was time to teach her unruly twins how to fish. Her first problem was to obtain their attention since they were either chasing butterflies, wrestling, or generally having a grand time. A few well placed cuffs along the side of the cubs' heads got their attention quickly. With the twins now paying full attention, the mother proceeded to show them how brown bears fish. Brown bear do not scoop fish out of a stream with their forepaws as black bear do. In deep water, brownies dive and grasp the salmon in their mouths. In shallow water, they fall on the fish with their forearms and then retrieve them into their mouths.

With a rush and a splash, the mother fell on a fish and came up with a coho salmon in her mouth. Upon showing it to the cubs, she dropped it back into the stream, indicating that they'd have to catch their own salmon. Somehow, those two cubs understood her message and got the word to go ahead. There was no attempt to search out a fish. They stood up with smart-aleck grins on their faces. I swear they said, "How'd I do, Mom?"

Well, she didn't like it. With a rush she was after them. They saw her barreling forward and rolled up into furry balls in the shallow water. Wham! She struck with her paws and they tumbled like wet basketballs. After stopping, they stood up whimpering like abused children asking, "Why'd you hit me, Mom?"

It was so comical one of us laughed out loud, followed by all of us. If we had blinked an eye, we would have missed the three of them heading for cover. A check of the empty river upstream told us our survey had come to an end.

With the anchor up, we were underway at once. Having set the course, I stayed at the wheel. I wasn't a member of the crew, but I would have not been very popular if I just sat around and watched the *hired help* work. Other than the cook, who was below fixing lunch, the three other fellows were sitting on the bench drinking coffee and smoking in the wheel house. It wasn't long before I thought I saw a disruption of some sort in the foot-high, choppy water some distance away. At first I thought it might be a big log. During high tides, it is common for beached logs to refloat and become a navigational problem. Later I thought I could occasionally see some water spout at intervals of possibly thirty seconds.

Hmm, I wondered. Could it be a whale? The crew had been having fun at my expense, pulling tricks on a dry-land farmer from North Dakota, so I was wary of exposing myself to more ridicule. Knowing that once a course has been confirmed by the captain, the helmsman must stay on course until the skipper changes it. With this in mind, I asked anyone in general if a whale is asleep and is dead-ahead of a ship, is it likely to be struck by the boat?

Don scoffed at the idea saying, "Don't worry. Whales can hear very well the thump, thump of the vessel's propeller under water. The whale will move out of the way."

The closer we came, the more positive I was that there was a sleeping whale in front of us. In plenty of time to turn safely off course, I said to Don, "Skipper! You had better take the wheel for I want you to be in command when we crash into this whale."

Thinking I was pulling his leg and not wanting to be taken in by it all but not being sure, he leisurely got up to stretch and looked around. Then seeing the whale he immediately grabbed the wheel and came hard left.

The monster slept on. That was one tired and sleepy whale. We cruised around it in a tight circle. We blew our whistle and even fired a rifle into the water alongside. The whale slept on. We finally tired of the game and continued on our course. From that time on the crew quit pulling tricks on me. Now I was an accepted member of the group.

THE WHITE RUSSIAN

AYLIGHT WAS FADING as we slowed our speed coming into Gull Cove. It was the fall of 1939. The patrol had gone real well so far.

I was now employed by the Alaska Game Commission as a wildlife agent. This was my first patrol on my own, that is. My breaking-in period had been spent working out of Petersburg with Howard Jensen and Hosea Sarber.

The crew of the *M.V. Bear* consisted of Captain Don Gallagher, engineer Chan Willard, deckhand George Gullifson, and the cook was Gordon Peterson. The *Bear* did not have pilot house controls, so Chan had to be in the engine room to answer the bells as they were rung down from the bridge by Don. There would be a *clang* from the bridge and then we could hear and feel Chan stopping the engine. It was so quiet and smooth that we could hear the gurgle as the bow parted the water. Don would time the speed just right. *Clang, clang, clang* for reverse then one *clang* for stop and we were right there, bow to the dolphin. A perfect landing. I wondered how many times Don had entered and made fast to the dolphin in Gull Cove. In less than two minutes George and I passed a slipline around the dolphin. We checked the line to see if it had enough slack to allow the ship to move up and down the piling as the tide ebbed and flowed. About then Don must have rung Chan off for the night and we all went below for the evening meal.

Gull Cove is in Icy Straits on Chichagof Island between Hoonah and Pelican City, across from Glacier Bay, Southeastern Alaska. This is an area of big, strong tides and an occasional iceberg floating out of Glacier Bay.

Radiophones installed on the Game Commission boats were a new thing. They were so new that the manual of instruction didn't come out until the following year. The A.C.S. (Alaska Communication System), which was Army, installed the sets and gave us instructions. We had to know what frequencies to listen to and which ones were for transmitting and the hours they could be used. As a rule we met their schedules and did pretty well for amateurs.

I had a 1900-hour schedule with the A.C.S. in Juneau. We seldom had a message from the head office but on this particular day the operator said, "We have a message for you. Can you copy?"

The signal was strong and I told him to go ahead. The text of the message was as follows,

> You are to proceed to Deer Harbor on Yakobi Island. There has been a shooting. The man shot was brought to Pelican City by a troller and airlifted to the Juneau Hospital. Investigate the shooting and if our information is correct, arrest the shooter, whom we understand to be an alien. As you know aliens cannot legally possess a firearm without a special permit. That alone is legal reason for making an arrest. Signature, Frank Dufresnene.

Up to now, working on the *M. V. Bear* had been kind of like playing — riding around in a big boat and slipping in and out of all the bays in a speedboat. By gosh, this was real. Shootings, aliens, and "Go get him?" Hey, I thought. I didn't contract for this, did I? This was the first I had heard about aliens and guns.

At this point the reader may be wondering why the Alaska Game Commission was in the business of arresting people for crimes other than game crimes. It so happened that the Alaska Game Commission was a federal agency when Alaska was a territory. Federal marshals and game agents were mighty thin in numbers, spread throughout all of Alaska. As a result, we were also deputy marshals and required to enforce the law. Oh, sure, I knew I had a badge but didn't really think I would ever be dispatched to arrest an alien who had shot someone.

The five of us were dumbfounded. We didn't know what to think, but we did know that our next destination was Deer Harbor. Luckily, I had been in Deer Harbor a couple of months before this incident with Howard Jensen. I knew that it was a small sheltered cove on the outer shore of Yakobi Island. The entrance to the cove comes directly from the open ocean through a narrow, shallow passageway. Trolling boats could enter and depart only on a half-tide or more. Our ship, the *Bear*, drew ten feet and could not safely enter the harbor. Fishermen often called the cove the gunkhole. This usually referred to a small, convenient, safe place to lay anchor away from the ocean. Deer Harbor fit that description perfectly. In the center of the bay was an anchored covered scow. An enterprising fellow had purchased this old fish-buyers' scow and converted it into a café. The trollers used it as a gathering place, relief from their lonesome trade. The owner, being a good businessman, had a short-wave radio for gathering news and entertaining his customers.

Upon entering the harbor, we were also quite aware that many fishermen had heard the message directed to me over the radiophones. Anyone with short wave at that time enjoyed learning the schedules of the various radiophone transmissions and listened in on a regular basis. It was easy to imagine what the fishermen holed up in Deer Harbor had planned for me to do in apprehending the shooter. Yes, it was easy for them.

After some discussion among the crew, it was agreed that our plan of attack would have to be decided after we arrived in the cove. So we cast off the slipline at 0500 hours and made the run to a small bight on the southeast of Yakobi Island. Breakfast was served en route so that George and I could depart as soon as it was light.

The weather was good, with a northerly wind helping to knock down the waves. About fifteen minutes after leaving the *Bear* in our speedboat, we felt the lift of the sea as we rounded the point into Cross Sound. From there on in it was a roller-coaster ride into Cross Sound — up and down the waves. One moment we were on top and could see all around, and the next moment we could see nothing but water. It was almost low water as we went over the bar at the entrance to the cove. Trollers were working the bay and many boats were anchored up as tight as swing room would allow. We could see an arm waving at us from an open window of the scow. I'm sure he was yelling at us, but even with the outboard at slow speed we couldn't hear him.

As we slid up alongside the scow we heard, "For God's sake! Keep your head down and come in through the hatch in the stern. Do you want to get shot?"

Did he say "shot"? I wondered. Believe me, we stayed low as we scampered into the scow through the stern entrance.

The cook and owner of the scow tried to recap the situation as best they could for my benefit.

The shooter, old John Mitcoff, was a White Russian who had escaped from Russia via Manchuria and China after the 1917 Revolution. Somehow he arrived at Deer Harbor some ten years earlier. He was single and something of a loner. Mitcoff spoke and understood English, but with a decided accent. A few years back he had moved ashore to a cabin in a small grove of trees. He had done very well trolling.

It was generally thought that he still had the first dollar that he had ever earned. Lacking a bank in the area, he kept his money in coffee cans buried in his backyard. Old John had been quiet and a good neighbor; no problem at all until that woman showed up. She came into the harbor with her man and in no time had bedded a number of fellows for a price. Within a short time she came ashore and moved in with John. Soon after this, her man came ashore and attempted to move in, too. It was quite obvious to John that the both of them were out to get everything that he had hidden in his backyard. So, John grabbed his rifle and ordered the man to leave. No doubt the guy thought John could be bluffed, so he jumped him.

Blam! Old John let go with his 30-30 and shot the guy in the upper chest/shoulder area. The man needed help but could still maneuver, so he and the woman took off in their boat.

"Old John must have gotten scared and upset and didn't know what to do, so he proceeded to hold everyone in the harbor hostage. All a person had to do was to go up on deck and Old John would let go with his 30-30. So far he hadn't hit anyone, but it had been mighty close at times."

The proprietor took another breath, and said, "So, what are you going to do about it?"

At that moment my head was in a whirl. What was I going to do about it? I worried. A very viable solution seemed to me to get the hell out of there and quit my job. For a moment I even thought about going back to work in the nice, safe mine, where people don't shoot at you, but was reminded by my crew of the situation that needed to be taken care of that very moment. If I had been older and more experienced I no doubt would have waited until nightfall to approach the beach. Possibly I would have gone ashore a good distance from John's cabin and slipped up on him silently. If worse came to worse, I could have burned him out of his cabin. Instead, George and I decided that the only action should be a frontal approach, right up the beach to his door. George was more than happy to stay at water's edge and tend the boat.

The tide was way out when the bow grounded on the beach. The big tides with a minus run-out made the walk up the beach about a quarter-of-a-mile. I checked the pistol in my shoulder holster and strode as boldly as I could on a straight line to the cabin. My heart was beating furiously. I was aware that every eye in the harbor was watching me. Frankly, I was scared. No shots were fired. I couldn't hear a sound. The door of the cabin was closed.

I stopped thirty to forty paces from the cabin and said, "John, I was sent here by the governor of Alaska." I paused for effect. "I was sent to talk to you. I want you to leave your rifle in the house and come out. You won't be harmed. No one will shoot you."

I waited. There was no movement or sound. I hoped that he had skipped out the back door and someone else would have to track him down. So I became braver.

"John, if you don't come out, I will not come in to get you. Instead, I will return to the government's big boat and radiophone for assistance. If this happens I can't guarantee what might happen. You might be shot or even killed. I believe that you should come out and talk to me. This is the best and safest way for you."

I heard a faint sound from inside the cabin and out John came. He was about 5 feet eight inches, 155 pounds, and appeared to be around fifty-five years old. You could tell that he was confused and bewildered by all that had been happening to him. I was already feeling sorry for him.

George and I went into his cabin to pick up his rifle and a few belongings before we left. As we headed out of the harbor with Old John, all of the fishermen came up on deck. They waved and tooted their horns as long as we were in sight.

We turned our prisoner over to the marshal in Hoonah that evening. I asked the marshall why I had been given the job.

"Well," he explained, "your boss said although they already had a boat in the vicinity, they wanted to see how their new, young agent operated under fire."

Yeah, thanks a lot, I thought.

I spent some time with the commissioner and marshal relating the circumstances that brought on the shooting. They agreed with me that a light, suspended sentence and the confiscation of his rifle were in order.

At dinner that night on board the *Bear*, Chan asked me, "Why did you take that damned-fool risk of getting shot? Landing on the beach right in front of Old John and then walking in plain sight right up to his cabin?"

I told Chan that I figured that John saw us enter the harbor. He could tell we weren't fishermen. Our boat was painted the U.S. Government color. We came into the harbor with just one stop at the scow to find out where he lived and then we came directly to the beach. I believed that he knew the injured man had made it to town and reported what happened to him. The gig was up for him!

Some time later we got some feedback on the incident. The consensus of the residents of Deer Harbor was that the young agent wasn't very smart, but he sure as hell was brave.

SITKA'S PIONEER HOME

W E ENTERED the channel between Sitka and Japonski Island and threaded our way Southward through the buoys past the Union Oil dock and the Sitka Cold Storage to the small boat harbor float. The Standard Oil dock and the Northland Transportation dock were next on the channel. It was September 1939 and my first visit to this area.

As you know, Sitka was the capital of Russian Alaska. Most likely they chose this site for a few reasons. Those reasons could have been that the westward parts of the Aleutians and Bristol Bay were very stark. Kodiak is quite far off the main part of Alaska, such as the Kenai Peninsula and Prince William Sound. The Kenai area has big tides and long shallow beaches. Sitka has deep waters and a direct entrance from the open sea. This must have been a major factor during those sailing ship days. The land is covered with a dense forest and the seas with fish. Sea otter and other fur-bearing animals were in abundance.

We had a couple of hours before dinner aboard the Game Commission vessel, the *M.V. Bear*, so we climbed the ramp from the float and headed into town. At the top of the ramp I was surprised to see a large, three-story building fronted by a groomed lawn. It was the Pioneer Home.

The Sitka Pioneer Home.

Gosh, I thought, I'll have to learn more about that place.

The Baranof Castle on my right was situated on a small rise with a view of the ocean on its south and west. Further down the street, in fact right in the middle of the street, was the St. Michael Russian Orthodox Church. The traffic to the east goes around the church on the water side, while the westbound skirts the church on the north side. What a grand setting for this lovely church.

At dinner I was pleased to learn that the skipper, Don Gallagher, knew the superintendent of the Pioneer Home, Einar Hansen, and intended to visit him that very night. It turned out that Einar was a long-time friend of Don's. Both of them had been born in Alaska and lived in Hoonah, Juneau, and various canneries. Einar had gone the route of schooling and management while Don had started crewing on boats at a young age and remained with the sea. All through dinner we talked about the old-timers who came to Alaska during the many gold rushes.

It is strange how we most often think of the gold rush days as being connected to the Klondike at and near Dawson. However, Alaska had many gold finds. Some were at Nome and Fairbanks, while two more were found in Candle; another was referred to as the Forty Mile. Even more confusing is the fact that most people consider the Klondike to be in Alaska when it is located in Canada's Yukon Territory.

A few of the thousands of men on these treks did make it big. However, most of them just made wages. Most of these thousands returned to the States. The others, most often, went from strike to strike ending up without families or funds to support them in their older years.

The first Pioneer Home was established by the territory for the express purpose of making a home for these wandering, adventurous old-timers. These are the men who climbed the Chilkoot and Dyea Pass, built boats and rafts, and ran the Yukon. Despite the hardships these men experienced, they retained their sense of humor and had fun. Proof can be found in the men's nicknames.

I recall some of the names and remember a few of the reasons for the names. The first one is easy: Swiftwater Charlie. He was named Swiftwater not because he was one of the pilots that, for a fee, would take crafts through the rapids on the Yukon, but because he was scared to death of the rapids. Many were called Slim, Shorty, or Fats. Often a man called Tiny was quite big. I recall there being a Dry Ole and a Wet Ole. One of these Oles drank. Kitchen Stove got his name while he was packing on the pass. It seemed that he contracted to carry a kitchen stove up and over the pass for a fee of a few dollars per pound. To everyone's delight, after establishing the weight of the pack, the owner slipped a sack of flour into the oven unseen. And then there was Sourdough Bill, Frozen Foot Johnson, Yukon Jake, Forty Mile Bill, Ramrod, and Moose. Two fellows with big feet were called Suitcase and Snowshoe. And, of course, Old Timers who were in Alaska prior to 1898 were called Sourdoughs. Everyone had a batch of sourdough at the back of the stove. Newcomers in 1898 and later were all called Cheechakos. My father-in-law, Ed Boyer, who went into the Klondike in 1898, was called Chauncey. I guess that there was a famous Englishman who dressed and acted the perfect gentleman. His name was Chauncey DePew. Ed always was a soft-spoken, well-dressed gentleman.

Don asked me if I would like to go with him on his visit to the home. I jumped at it. We met Einar at the home and were shown about the place. Oh, how I wanted to hear the stories these old-timers could tell. Most of the men were in pretty good shape and enjoyed themselves. However, they were bound to get bored, for one can only read so much, play pool so long, and deal cards so often. The home saw to it that each man received pocket money for smokes and personal items. But, it had to be limited. Otherwise there would be a bunch of drunks on their hands.

Over a cup of coffee at the home, Einar told us of a real concern. He and his staff were worried and at a loss to explain the increased number of deaths. Actuarial studies on the expected deaths of the home residents had proved to be correct until of late. Now these old guys were dropping like flies. We talked of other things but I kept thinking back to the problem that Einar had shared.

After leaving the home, Don and I dropped by the Sitka bar for a "nightcap" — anything to keep from going back to the ship right away. We planned on having only one drink, so we nursed it. A number of old-timers from the home were sitting around, talking and smoking but not drinking. Being idle and interested in their chatter, I was aware of a man at the bar leaving his half-finished drink to go to the restroom. Quickly, one of the old-timers slipped up to the bar and downed the drink. When the man returned from the men's room, everyone was in their place as before.

"Hmm," the man must have considered, "I thought I had some of my drink left. Guess not, think I'll have another one."

I had to smile. Good for the old-timer. The same drama was reinacted a number of times. I left part of my drink for one of the quick-drink artists.

Our next patrol found us making fast to the float in Sitka almost two months to the day from our last call. That evening Don and I again visited with Einar Hansen. He could hardly wait for us to sit down to tell us the good news. One of his staff had found the solution to the mystery of the untimely deaths of the old-timers.

One of the old-timers at the home had set up a raffle. Tickets were sold at a buck a piece. Each man made a guess as to which one of his friends would die next. The winner was the one who correctly guessed who would die next. This winner would be suddenly and secretly rich! At his own pace, the new rich would drink too much, not eat enough, and end up on the marble slab. The next winner would proceed to follow his friend to the grave. Some of the winners would go right out and get dead drunk and end up in the rain passed out. Often, he would be dead within twenty-four hours of winning. And so it went.

Einar and his staff, upon breaking the code, gathered everyone in the dining room and held them there while all of the rooms were searched. Next, all of the old guys were searched and raffle tickets taken. Knowing what to look for, the raffle was kept in check. Once more, Einar said they were back to the actuarial expected deaths.

Einar explained the lottery. "Hell, those guys are just sitting around waiting to die. They've lived pretty wild, adventuresome lives. They have nothing to lose. A few months or years living at the home isn't really quality living."

" 'What the heck,' " they'd say to themselves. "'I'm rich! I'll live it up big and check out in a blaze of glory.' "

A RAINBOW

ICY STRAITS, 1939

R AINBOWS never fail to mesmerize me. And I find it interesting that most rainbows are far away, often faint and usually not complete from ground level on one side to the other. You're a lucky dog if you glimpse a double rainbow.

We were cruising on the *M. V. Bear* in Icy Straits heading east. The mainland and Glacier Bay were on our left to the north, and Chichagof Island, with the Indian village of Hoonah, to the south. The rainy weather had changed to partly cloudy and a few sunbreaks appeared here and there. The five of us were up in the pilot house enjoying the pleasant weather and calm seas. To our amazement, a beautiful rainbow appeared in the distance. One end of the rainbow anchored at water level, approximately three miles in front of us. As we approached the end of the rainbow, it seemed to stay in place rather than retreat as we advanced.

We joked about the possibility of finding a pot of gold, but realized that the water was 120 fathoms deep — an impossible depth to reach the elusive gold fabled to be at the end of a rainbow! The rainbow stayed in place. George, the deckhand, and I went out on the foredeck to see what would happen. Soon the boat was inside the rainbow. The many colors were all about us as though we were in a giant kaleidoscope. I looked at George and the rainbow colors were little speckles all over him. I put out my hands and arms and the colors were all over me. If only we had some beautiful music playing we might have thought that we were in heaven! I don't recall how long we were in that beautiful, colored and speckled light. I remember that we didn't even speak to each other, afraid to break this spell. We were numb and in awe.

The crew was curious as to whether or not the skipper would record this in the logbook, since it was his responsibility to record all such observations and activity. His remark was, "Hell no, I'm not going to put it in the logbook. Who would believe it?"

I certainly did, but no one back in port would.

TRACY ARM

W E DEPARTED before dawn for the six-hour run from Juneau to Tracy Arm. The February sky was clear with many stars. The north wind told us that the weather would be cold and clear, perfect for the trip's purpose: to take movie and still pictures of mountain goats in their winter habitat. Of the six of us aboard the Alaska Game Commission boat, the *M.V. Bear*, five of us were employees and the sixth was Malcolm Grainey, a professional photographer. Malcolm had been with us during the previous August at Pack Creek on Admiralty Island when we watched the hilarious episode of a mother brown bear attempting to teach her uncooperative twins how to catch salmon.

At breakfast he reminded us that he was not part of the crew and should not be expected to assist in any of the duties involving the operation of the boat. At all times he must be focused on picture taking; otherwise a rare picture opportunity might be missed.

Tracy Arm is on the mainland, south of Juneau on Stephens Passage and across from the Glass Peninsula. It is a spectacular, beautiful area to visit, with steep cliffs, glaciers, floating ice, seals, and sea birds.

Upon entering the inlet and before reaching the steep area where we hoped to see mountain goats, Malcolm set up two tripods and mounted 35mm and 16mm cameras. I was checked out to operate the 16mm camera. Malcolm also had a couple of cameras and a light meter hanging from his neck. Believe me, we were all set to take close-up and also telephoto pictures.

Exploring the Tracy Arm with camera.

Prior to leaving the low-laying land, Don Gallagher, the skipper, explained some things that I was not familiar with.

"As a rule, the way the land appears to be is pretty much the way the area under water will be. For example, you can figure that the low land on our left will result in shallow water out in front. I'll run the boat over to the cliff up ahead where the almost vertical incline will continue down into the water."

With that, he piloted the boat up close to the shore and nudged the bow against the cliff. At an extremely slow speed we skirted the north side about sixty to ninety feet off shore. Soon the cliff was at least 3,000 feet high and at an angle of sixty-five to ninety degrees. Almost at once, we could see goats half way up and higher. These long shots were good to have, but of course we hoped to see some much closer.

102

Moderate waves began to rock the boat. The next turn brought a large glacier into view. Huge chunks of ice fell off the face of the glacier into the water.

Don said, "The big tides lifting under the overhanging glacier contribute to the excessive floating ice."

Although the hull of the boat was protected at water's edge with iron bark, the skipper rang "stop the engines" to avoid striking the ice any harder than necessary. Once a vessel is underway, it will proceed without power for a good distance just by virtue of its weight and momentum. We rounded a small point and surprised three goats at water's edge. They were unaware of our silent approach until Don rang "full astern" to stop the boat's forward motion. The sound of the prop wash

Mountain goats on the hillside at Tracy Arm.

and the blast from the stack really got their attention. They appeared to be a family of three, come down low to lick salt off the rocks. This seemed unusual to me since females and kids herd up higher together at this time of the year while the males go it alone. Yes, the three consisted of a billy, a nanny, and a kid. We held our collective breaths wondering what would happen. Contrary to stories you may have heard, goats don't run and leap from crag to crag in steep, dangerous country. A number of goats are killed every year due to falls and avalanches.

The billy stood on his hind legs and extended his body searching with his front hooves for a foothold. He found a tiny ledge and pulled himself up. It was so small we couldn't even see the ledge from the boat, The billy goat hurried along to our right no doubt searching for the next step up. The baby goat repeatedly scampered up the rock face only to slide back down. The poor little thing was so frightened it kept making a little bleating sound. To our utter amazement, the mother goat placed her head under the baby's rump and pushed it up to the ledge. In the meantime, the billy had located another higher-up ledge. And so they climbed, the billy finding and leading the way, the nanny pushing the kid up the cliff. Time seemed to stand still while we watched this unusual happening.

After the goats were much higher on the cliff and the trance was broken, I asked Malcolm, "Did you get some spectacular pictures?"

"You know," he said, "I was so mesmerized with what was happening that I didn't get a single picture. Now, isn't that a heck of a note?"

THE KING OF THE TRAPPERS

THE NUSHAGAK AND MULCHATNA RIVERS, 1940

THE FIRST NIGHT of our patrol up the Nushagak and Mulchatna Rivers was spent on our outboard riverboat at Ekwok. The boat was 18 feet long, covered bow to past midship with a tarp secured to the bow, and slanted upward to allow headroom in a kneeling position. We slept and cooked under the tarp.

The Alaska Game Commission had sent me from Juneau to the Bristol Bay area of Alaska to assist "Two-Gun Carson" with the spring beaver sealing. In retrospect, I believe it was to have been my introduction to the outback country, eventually to being stationed there. Talk about isolated! Nome, Bethel, Barrow, or Kotzebue didn't have anything on Dillingham, Naknek, or Kanakanak. Up until a few years ago, with the advent of better airplanes, the only means of transportation to this area was by boat. During the winter months, the Bering Sea froze solid. So if you didn't want to get stuck there until spring, you made the last sailing in the fall. If you stayed the winter in one of those villages, it was mighty grim. Today the tiny towns have good radio, movies, and earth stations to bring in television from satellites, plus daily mail service and jets to Anchorage.

Two-Gun's real name was Carlos. He claimed to be a direct descendent of the famous Kit Carson. He was married to a short, squat, humorless, hard-working, almost ugly woman. I don't know much about her, since our conversations consisted of, "Pass the butter, please," and "No, thank you."

Above: Our boat moored at the causeway; below: Jack in the boat.

Possibly the longest verbal exchange between us was, "Goodbye, we'll see you when we get back."

Carlos had been nicknamed Two-Gun by the other agents. His only reading material was "true detective" stories. Unlike the other agents, who wore a shoulder holster gun hidden under a jacket, he wore two guns hung at his waist.

One of the passages that he liked best in the stories that he read was, "If you feel lucky, go for your guns." The other passage related to the federal agents of the FBI and CIA since he, too, was a federal agent.

Carson starting the outboard

This passage involved a very tight situation encountered by a lone federal agent while he was surrounded by the bad guys. He would take a firm stand, spread his hands ready to go for his guns, while most likely also going to his death with guns blazing. He would say, "Remember, men, where one federal agent falls, three more will take his place."

He really liked that brave stand. He actually got so that he believed it. It was pretty heady stuff.

The Nushagak, being a big river, was still ice-locked, so we did our job in the Naknek and Kvichok area first. Ekwok is a small native village. Despite its distance overland from Bristol Bay, the tide ebbs and flows to a few miles upriver from the village. The villagers consisted of a mixture of Indians and Eskimos, plus one white family. The one white man fished the red salmon run in the bay and lived at Ekwok for the remainder of the year as an unaffiliated missionary. He impressed me

*Village along the
Nushagak River.*

*Elevated Nushagak
River village.*

108

with his true sense of service to the community. He didn't take up a collection at the Sunday services thus not siphoning off money from the congregation. His was a free service to the villagers. When he first arrived at Ekwok, the toilet facilities for the village were the tide flats. With his own funds, he purchased a small sawmill. With the help of willing villagers, they felled and sawed trees and constructed outhouses. Soon new and better dwellings were built. Then they constructed a pretty, little log church. I attended Sunday services in that church. It was great fun to see the villagers sitting on benches in their parkas. I recall one sermon relating a story about the test of the sun against the wind to see which could make them remove their parkas. The missionary's contribution to the village was even more remarkable when one realized there were no trees around or near Dillingham or Naknek. Only inland and at a higher level could trees be cut.

Ours was a slow pace traveling upriver. We stopped at numerous small camps and villages sealing winter-caught beaver skins and helping the people in various ways. We showed them a new way to stretch beaver skins to make them more valuable to fur buyers.

My first exposure to a different culture was at the next village above Ekwok. The homes were built on high ground to avoid flooding in the spring. We beached our boat and took the trail to high ground. I was leading the way when I saw a woman squatting in the grass alongside the path. I turned to Carson waiting to see what we should do.

He said, "These people have no false modesty. Relieving oneself is natural and normal. As you pass her, just smile and say, 'Hello.'"

She responded to my smile with, "Chumia." I said the same to her. We continued on into the village. Apparently I was the only one embarrassed.

In the spring, the men came downriver to sell their winter-caught furs and many of the families remained at home. To the children who never came to town, a white man was an oddity. We were probably the first for many of them. For the families who do accompany the men, standard procedure was for the men to get drunk. The women and children would then ride the one and only taxi five miles to Kanakanak and back. At that time, this stretch of road from Dillingham to Kanakanak was the only one in the entire Bristol Bay area.

I didn't know until we came to the confluence of the Nushagak and the Mulchatna that we had a specific destination and purpose on this patrol. Carlos told me that it was rumored the King had four men with him. He ran a strict no-nonsense camp with no women to cause dissension. Five dog teams with long traplines and way-cabins along the way was the rule.

The law allowed each person to trap and have in his possession ten beaver skins. The rumor was that the King and his men trapped out an area and then moved to a new place each year. It was also rumored that they possessed many illegal beaver skins. We were situated at the perfect spot to catch them with the goods. No doubt their plan was to cache the surplus skins further downriver, then return to pick them up after being cleared in Dillingham.

At that time, the bay area (Bristol Bay) and the north country were known as hideaway places for hundreds, maybe thousands of men who had escaped from civilization. Jailbirds were looking for another chance. Men who had evaded the law, a wife, or the responsibilities of a regulated life ended up in the bay area, most often under an assumed name. Birth certificates and Social Security numbers were only for the gainfully

Beaver skins.

employed. From the sound of things, the King qualified as a charter member of the club.

On the third day around noon, we heard dog noises far upriver. Soon the dogs could be heard more clearly, and then the boats came around the bend of the Mulchatna—five boats in all. Each boat was tarped over from the bow to about midship, where the dogs were all kept. The entrance of the Mulchatna to the big river was at a direct 90 degree angle. Even had they wanted to, the boats could not have avoided floating straight across to where we were. Carson stood up on the bank yelling and pointing for them to beach their boats. I felt like I was in a movie. Each man beached his boat in what looked like a prearranged maneuver. After the boats were secure, each man then stepped ashore and stood at the bow of his boat with his 30-30 rifle at the ready.

The King was a big man. I would guess that he was about 6 feet 2 inches, 215 pounds, and around forty-five years of age. The other men ranged from about 5 feet 8 inches to 6 feet, and twenty-five to forty years of age. They were all flat-bellied and hard as nails from a winter of snow-shoeing and running behind their dogs. They looked like they could chew up spikes and spit out shingle nails.

There was a long silence before Carson spoke.

He said, "We are United States Federal Wildlife Agents. We have reason to believe that you men have many illegal beaver skins. We are authorized by the U.S. Government to board and search any boat. So step aside while we search your boats."

The King replied, "First off, nobody's going to come aboard any of our boats unless we tell them that they can. Secondly, we have not broken any law and we don't have any illegal beaver skins."

I began to realize that these guys could kill us and sink our boat. The only law in the entire area was the fat-bellied, over-aged U.S. Marshal who hadn't been out of Dillingham for ten years.

Two Gun is going to get us killed, I thought.

Then I heard Carson say, "Remember, we are federal officers. Where one federal officer falls, three or more will stand in his stead."

Flipping back his jacket to expose his two guns and taking a gunslinger's stance, he said, "If you feel lucky, go for your guns."

"Well, well, I'm not going to kill a man over this silly thing," said the King. "Go ahead and search us."

You guessed it. They were perfectly legal. That did it. I returned to Juneau as fast as I could.

MY TRIP TO THE WRONG-WAY-HOME PEOPLE

ALEGNAGIK, 1941

IT WAS April 1941 when I arrived in Anchorage from Juneau via the passenger ship *S.S. Denali* and the Alaska Railroad from Seward. My destination was Dillingham in Bristol Bay to assist Wildlife Agent Don "Two Gun" Carson during the beaver sealing period. We were both with the Alaska Game Commission, a federal agency, since Alaska was still a territory. Although, I had lived in Juneau since 1935, this was my first trip west. I was young and everything was exciting, fun, and different.

The first night out of Juneau on the *S.S. Denali*, I had a little problem with my roommate. The two of us, total strangers, were assigned a minimum-class room on B deck. This meant that we each had a bunk and a shared wash basin. The facilities were down the hall and around the corner.

During the night, I was awakened by the click of his bunk light. With eyes half-closed, I watched him in interest wondering what he was up to. He went over to the wash basin and stood there and soon I could hear the tinkle of water running.

In utter amazement I asked him, "Hey, what are you doing?"

He replied, "Well, what in the hell does it look like?"

I shuddered at the thought of having to wash my face in that basin, so in the morning the purser moved me to a room by myself on C deck.

This was one level below B Deck. It had a porthole and the steward told me that it was okay to open the porthole during good weather and when we were inside. But when out in the gulf, "Do not open the porthole!"

After he left, I looked out and saw that the water was smooth, so I immediately opened the port. The fresh air was great! It was fun lying in my bunk reading, taking it easy, and feeling the movement of the ship. Possibly a half-hour later, I suddenly was gasping and sputtering because the ship had taken a roll and submerged my open porthole. I put on dry clothes and moved across the room to a dry bunk and worried about how I would cope with the steward when he saw the mess I'd made.

The next morning I took the 7:30 A.M. train for the five-hour ride to Anchorage—a great trip through the mountains and over high wooden trestles, and through a number of tunnels. The engineer blew the engine whistle whenever he sighted moose, and we chased one down the tracks. This added to the fun and excitement of the trip. Hotel rooms were difficult to obtain, so I slept at the City Fire Hall. Crazy!

The snow was gone in the lowlands in the Anchorage area. The lakes, however, were frozen. Over on the Bristol Bay side, it was still winter. The plan was to take off from Lake Hood on skis and land in the snow at Dillingham. The weather was bad until April 11th. The waiting time was spent helping around the office sealing beaver skins. The wait was difficult for me because I wanted to get going.

On April 11th we took off in a Bristol Bay Air Service plane on skis. Our destination was Dillingham. Johnny Walatka was the pilot. Soon, it was snowing and blowing. The only incident en route up the pass was the sudden glimpse of a plane flashing past us traveling in the opposite direction. He was over to our right about twenty feet and about fifty feet above us or we would all have been statistics. Johnny said it was a Star Airline plane and the flyer was Sasse. Since our plane could not climb high enough to go over the top, it was necessary to cross the mountains through the pass. We got as far as the Lake Clark Glacier and there we were stalled. It appeared that a glacier came down the mountain on each side and with the wind and snow, the pilot couldn't tell clouds from ice and snow. Without the visual see through, we could not shoot the pass.

Just below the glacier there is a bowl-like area that made it possible to circle repeatedly. On occasion, you could see horizon through the gap, but by the time we got up to the pass again the curtain would shut down. We circled and circled. A soldier with the Alaska Communication System, who was being transferred to Kanakanak — Do you realize this name spells the same frontward as well as backward? — was the passenger seated behind me. Hearing an unusual sound, I raised up and turned to get a look. His cheeks were extended similar to the way one blows up a balloon. At that moment, he became ill all over the back of the seat and me.

Gad, I thought. Me and my curiosity!

The smell was pretty strong. Soon we had to retreat while our gasoline supply held out. Finally, back over Anchorage, the air was smooth— making the soldier's recovery possible.

Glancing out of the window and seeing buildings, he asked me, "Is that Kanakanak?"

"No," I said, "that's Anchorage."

He replied, "Oh, my God! I went through all of that and I'm back in Anchorage!"

At that time, servicemen could refuse to fly. If he held to his promise, they would keep a place for him until a passenger ship was available, possibly not until later in the spring. Then he would make the long boat trip around Unamak Pass. If he thought those few hours of airsickness were difficult, just wait until the seasickness set in for a few days. Poor fellow, I never knew how he made out.

April 12th, 13th, and the 14th brought more bad weather and a longer wait in Anchorage. On the 14th, Gren Collins, a flying game warden, asked me if I'd like to take a little flight. Of course I did. So, we took off on skis and circled about for some time enjoying the scenery.

Gren casually said, "You possibly noticed the ice on the lake is a mess. We don't have pontoons for this plane so we are going to have to go to wheels. Do you mind if I land on Merrell Field?"

I was the added weight he felt he needed to make this dry dirt landing on skis. I was in a spot, so of course I said, "Sure, let's do it."

Skis are terribly noisy on normal landings. You should hear skis on dry dirt and gravel. He came in as slow as he dared and held it on the prop as long as he could, and then yelled "Hang on!" and cut the throttle.

We rocked violently, forward and back, but didn't flip over. The prop happened to be in the wrong position and was broken. For my second time on skis, that was a pretty thrilling landing.

Johnny's plane was now on pontoons awaiting the final decay of the ice. I can't believe that it happened so fast, but my notes state, "April 15th — still awaiting weather and final rotting of the ice. April 16th, we took off at 12:45 P.M. on pontoons with a good weather report at Dillingham. It's approximately 375 miles overland to Bristol Bay. This was to be my longest flight to date.

I recall thinking Lindbergh flew across the Atlantic with wheels, and there we were flying over land with pontoons.

Johnny's float plane on Lake Aleknagik.

Once on the other side of the pass, we dropped down to the low lands and followed the Nushagak River. The river was frozen over. About now I began to worry about our landing at Dillingham. Nushagak Bay was not frozen over but my notes said, "Arrived at the bay about 5 P.M. There was a great deal of ice in the river. The tide was still flooding, pushing the ice against the shore and cluttering the usually open water."

I was up front with Johnny and he, seeing my concern, said, "Don't worry, kid. I know a spot where we can land until the tide changes."

With that, he headed north up the Wood River. Soon we flashed over open water at the outlet of this lake. Johnny yelled at me over the roar of the engine, "That's Lake Aleknagik."

Up ahead, I saw my first working Alaskan dog team coming across the lake ice toward the south shore. Landing handily on the water and staying on the step, Johnny taxied over to the beach. Much to my surprise, I saw cabins up in the trees and people hurrying down to the lake's shore.

About this time I started to have an odd feeling. Without question I'd never been here. The people were strangers, but somehow I felt I knew them. Suddenly I believed I had the answer. I dug around in my

Dog sled along the shore.

pack and unearthed a copy of the *Saturday Evening Post* dated April 12, l941. (Magazines print their copies early and ship them out ahead of time; thus, the April 12th date and my having it there on April 16th). This issue carried an article with pictures of "The Pioneers of Wrong-Way-Home" by Herbert H. Hilscher. Mr. Hilscher had visited this settlement in October, 1940. The settlement at Alegnagik couldn't have received a copy any faster if it had been via special delivery. The people knew Mr. Hilscher had taken pictures and intended to write an article for publication. But of course they had no idea that it had been published and in a national magazine.

My, what fun it was to give my copy to those people. You can well imagine the excitement that this article brought to the settlement. As the issue was passed from hand to hand you could hear, "There's Betty! Look, the entire Smith family having dinner!"

And so it went. I recall names like Ray Smith, Lloyd and Myron Moody, Jim Putvin, and the Hoffman's.

This settlement started in the 1930s with just the Ray Smith family. They came up the river and pitched a tent and lived in it until the log cabin was completed. Betty Smith McCluskey was born that December in this first cabin. The Moody's and other children followed. It is truly a story of hardship and bravery. They did it all by themselves with no governmental help.

It was dinner time. Johnny and his five passengers were invited to eat with them. It appeared that they had enough food for six extra people on a moment's notice. My guess is that some of them had meager portions that night in order to extend their hospitality. Roast moose, potatoes, and canned peas comprised the main course I recall.

The tide had changed and amid many "thank-yous" and "goodbyes" we took off and headed south. The landing at Dillingham was tricky, but Johnny handled it like he did this all of the time. There were still chunks of ice in the water. We made a run downwind to look over the landing area. I couldn't see enough water to accommodate us, but Johnny swung around and proceeded to land just the same. Once down, he kept the stick ahead and taxied under power on the step. The first ice sheet showed up in front of us with clear water for only one pontoon. A deft movement of the controls and the right pontoon came out of the water. We "stepped" like that: first one pontoon and then the other, until he cut the throttle at the beach. Once our forward speed had slowed, Johnny gave the engine the throttle again and up the muddy beach we proceeded, just like skis on snow. Frankly, I didn't know a pontooned airplane could do this. Up the beach we progressed until, at high water mark, there was an extra surge of power, and the plane swung around and stopped. At last, I had arrived at Dillingham.

Oh, yes, I was so very curious as to the name "Wrong-Way-Home." Mr. Hilscher had entitled his story, "The Pioneers of Wrong-Way-Home." I am sure he explained the title in his story but I had forgotten. I wrote to Betty Smith McCluskey (who was ten years old at the time we made our unannounced visit) and asked her the question. She wrote back with this explanation.

During stormy weather, with fog or snow and visibility being poor, the natives often mistook the mouth of the Wood River for the Nushagak River. They would continue up the river until they came to the first lake. It would be then when they discovered their mistake, and they would shout in disgust and anger, "Aleknagik!" This means, of course, "Wrong way home!"

IT WAS A MYSTERY

I T WAS IN JULY 1941 that I accepted a position as wharfinger in Sitka with the Northland Transportation Company. A wharfinger is a manager of a dock or wharf. Northland, one of the three American steamship firms serving Alaska, was referred to as the middle one. The Alaska Steamship Company was the big one while the Alaska Transportation Company was the smallest. Around the end of the war, the Alaska Steamship Company bought out Northland.

I went ahead to Sitka on the *S.S. North Sea* since we knew that housing was in very short supply. Actually, let me rephrase that: there were no homes to be found. The Sitka Naval Air Station was far from being completed and there was an air of urgency about the job. I did locate a house to rent and it was made available to us only because I was classed as a likely permanent resident. It was a horrid little place to which I brought Ann upon the arrival of her boat from Juneau. We had lived in Juneau for six years. Those years were such happy times for Ann — a nice home, good friends — and now she was being uprooted again.

I don't know what feature of the house bothered Ann the most. Could it be the oil heater situated in the middle of the room and how it only worked half of the time? Or, was it having to wash clothes in the bathtub on the second floor? Possibly, it was the tiny bedroom. One had to enter the bed from the foot and climb up, then crawl your way to the head of the bed. Or, maybe it was the worn-out floor covering that continually dirtied our daughter Janis as she crawled about. Or, the rain that never stopped making it difficult to shop. And no car. After roughing it for two months, we moved closer to downtown and the docks into the DeArmond house.

The DeArmond house was old. It had high ceilings — ten to twelve feet high. We had the downstairs section of the house. Mrs. DeArmond, a newly married couple, and a single lady who was a waitress in the Sitka Café, all lived upstairs. We never knew how the upstairs was arranged for the four people.

The directions on how to find the house were quite simple: walk up from the Northland dock past Pros Ganty's store with the Pioneer Home on your left. Turn at the next narrow street going to your left (north) and walk up to the end of the street. From here, you will see a long boardwalk — possibly 100 yards — that will lead you to the front door of the DeArmond House.

The DeArmond House today.

Upon arrival, our immediate thought would be, "I wonder if the Russians built this house when Sitka was the Capital of Alaska?"

When I saw this long board walk, I had two thoughts at once: "This is going to be a drag packing stuff up and down the walk. And the oil man must have a long hose to pump stove oil to the tank."

In Juneau, it was common to see oil being delivered to homes perched on the mountainside with no roads, only stairs.

Outside the back door was a huge tank. It seemed that it might hold about 1,000 gallons. I settled up with the man who moved out by paying him for the oil remaining in the tank. Inside the kitchen door, hanging on a nail, was a calibrated stick used to determine the amount of oil in the tank. A chart on the wall gave the gallons by referring to the figures on the stick. As I recall, there were about 500 gallons left in the tank. So we had lots of oil and I didn't have to worry about having the tank fueled for a good period of time. Since we had no idea how much oil was burned in a month, I checked the tank and learned that after a month we had 600 gallons. This seemed ludicrous since we started with 500. But we were busy and thought that somehow we had been mistaken. Two months later, I gave it a check and much to my amazement, the oil was almost up to the top of the filler plug. I could only think how strange it was that the tank was filled without having ordered it. Possibly it was always filled at certain dates.

The Standard Oil Dock was right next to our dock. A few days later I took the occasion to ask how the delivery of oil was planned for regular customers. The man asked me, "Are you thinking about the house that you live in?"

"Yes, I was," I told him.

"We do not deliver to the DeArmond House."

So, I called the Union Oil Dock, the only other oil supplier in Sitka.

"Mr. Jeffrey, we do not deliver oil to the DeArmond House."

That night I told Ann the problem. Our problem was that we were going to have to start draining the oil out of the tank before it started running out on the ground. If we only had a road up to the house, people could come in pick-up trucks and cart it away. We had fun joking about having an oil well, but it still seemed pretty peculiar and a bit worrisome.

Pros Gantly, an old-timer in town, told me that Jack Conway would most likely know the answer to my oil well problem. So I called Jack at the Union Oil Dock. I asked him, "Jack, do you know how oil is delivered to the DeArmond House?"

He said, "I sure do!" and told me this bit of history.

When the Pioneer Home was being built, they wanted the cheapest rate for their oil to be delivered through a pipeline. His outfit was the lowest bidder. Mr. DeArmond agreed to their laying the pipe across his land, if they would put a tee in the pipe and deliver him oil. This was done.

The delivery to the DeArmond home was programmed as follows: Check the gallons in the tank. Yell, "Turn her on." When the tank was almost full, they would yell, "Turn her off."

The gallons delivered would be deducted from the Pioneer Home's bill.

"Well, Jack," I said, "the valve is leaking oil through to the tank and it's almost full."

"Okay," he said, "I'll turn her off, and say, let's forget about the amount of oil that has leaked through. After all, how could we know the correct amount?"

It was nice to solve that mystery.

A Happening at the Baranof Castle

Sitka, 1941

Russia sold Alaska to the United States in 1867. It was at Sitka that the Russian flag was hauled down and the American flag flown in its place. Secretary of State Seward had arranged the purchase of Alaska, and it was often referred to as "Seward's Folly." Sitka was the capital of the Territory of Alaska until 1906 when it was moved to Juneau.

Lord Baranof was in charge of the Russian forces as they progressed to the east, down the Aleutian Island chain to the mainland of Alaska, and on to Kodiak Island. Sea otter pelts were of great value, especially to the Chinese, and the local Indians were recruited to assist in the harvest. It was at Sitka, the last headquarters of the Russians, where Baranof built his home, called the Baranof Castle.

We moved to Sitka in 1941 where I was employed as the Northland Transportation Company's wharfinger, or dock operator. By early fall, we were established in the DeArmond home, located not far from the docks and the central part of town. On December 7, a Sunday, we were blessed with a clear sky, sunshine, and best of all, no rain. Radio transmissions were very poor, so we seldom tried our radio until nightfall. It was while we were strolling on the main street that we heard of the Japanese attack on Pearl Harbor.

The Baranof Castle (on hill at left) and Sitka in 1885. Courtesy of the Alaska State Library, Early Prints of Alaska, PCA 01-2199.

We were shocked. It was hard to believe. But quickly, we learned that strict wartime measures for safety would need to be followed. Now we would have to practice measures like dimming lights on automobiles, as well as homes, and covering all the windows in our home. There was a small contingent of sailors on the Sitka Naval Air Base. The first night the sailors were instructed to shoot out any windows of people who were found unwilling to follow the covered window measure. No windows were shot out, but there was that threat.

Construction to expand the naval base began immediately, even though most civilians felt that there was little likelihood of an invasion. Then, on June 3, 1942, Japanese forces bombed Dutch Harbor's Base, with some lives lost.

"Who was next?" we all wondered. Soon after, the Navy called the Sitka townspeople together to discuss the war effort and to ask for civilian assistance when and where it was needed. It was explained that Sitka and the Naval Air Base might be subjected to what they referred to as

"Japanese Flash Attacks." With the open sea so close, a ship or submarine might lay offshore and fire rounds of shells into the town. Most likely, the attack would be after dark in the dead of night, and could involve frogmen swimming ashore to investigate the town and base. The Naval officers went on to tell us that they were in the process of establishing a lookout station on the mountain behind Sitka. Its location would be below the normal cloud cover, but high enough to observe at least fifteen miles out to sea. Being short on troops, the officers asked for volunteers to assist on this project. There was an immediate show of hands, mine among them.

As it turned out, we had enough volunteers, whereby we would only have to serve three hours, one night a week. I signed up for the hours of 2 A.M. to 5 A.M. on Sunday mornings, so I would be free to handle the cargo and passenger ships while they were in port. This turned out to be easy duty, as there really wasn't anything for us to do. We met in the Power House downtown office for duty where we had a direct phone connection with the lookout on the mountain. Off and on, they

Rear view of the Baranof Castle in 1889. Photo by W.H. Case, courtesy of the Alaska State Library, Early Prints of Alaska, PCA 01-3451.

127

would call down to the office advising us of no action. Most often, we would fall asleep until our shift was over. On clear nights, we did some patrolling of the downtown streets.

Other volunteers were called into service. Bob Ellis was one. Bob had been a commercial flier in Ketchikan and a graduate of Annapolis. He flew his float plane to Sitka. At that time, he was the only pilot and had the only plane for the Sitka Naval Air Base. With a bomb lashed behind the front seat and opposite the righthand door, Bob was all set to patrol the ocean west of Sitka.

One day, he sighted what looked like a submarine in the water. His assistant undid the lashings, and steadied the bomb until Bob was over the target. Raising the plane's left wing, and with the door open it was "Bombs away!"

It was a strike.

It was a whale!

About 3 A.M. one morning, the phone rang at the Power House. I answered it and the lookout person said, "There appears to be some sort of signal showing from the Baranof Castle. I'm a signal man but I certainly can't read these. I suppose that you guys should check it out."

It might help the reader to understand that the castle was empty and used only as a stop for tourists.

Well, I thought. Maybe there was something important going on at the castle. Perhaps, some frogmen had come ashore after all. Certainly these men would be highly trained and have superior weapons that would easily outgun the four of us civilians on duty. One of us had a shotgun, two had .45s, and I had my shoulder-holstered short-barreled .22 pistol. What should we do? The other fellows had awakened with the phone call and began discussing the situation. We planned our strategy and decided to sneak up on the Baranof from four sides to see what was happening. For sure, it was best to take it slow, given that it was totally dark, and we agreed that it was also intelligent to not charge up the small hill in our excitement.

The wind had picked up to gale force and the rain was coming down sideways from the southwest. I called the lookout and advised him of our plan and asked for backup.

"If you hear shots fired, get some troops over there fast. We won't challenge the enemy, but will be hiding out and observing. The enemy might head for the beach in an attempt to return to their vessel."

I chose the east side of the small hill where Baranof Castle was located, and the others chose their side. Each man had a flashlight and a watch. It was agreed that we would be in our observation spot and make our move up the small incline at 3:30 A.M. We took off into the wind and rain. It was a wild night! Seeing where you were going without checking with a covered light made going difficult. At exactly 3:30 A.M., I started up the incline. In no time I was in position where I could see across the grounds to the building. Actually, I could see very little given the darkness and the amount of rain coming down. Suddenly, there was a flash of light! I ducked down. Then, there were two or three more flashes. This went on for some time. Some flashes were rapid, and others held. I imagined a set of dots and dashes, but none of them seemed to follow a pattern. There was no sound except for the huge gusts of wind and falling rain.

One of our guys looked to be braver than the rest of us. Through the flashes I could see him crawling across the open area. I held my breath and worried for his safety. Luckily, no shots and no other sounds. Then, I noticed the fellow from the north side crawling toward the castle.

More flashes of light! It was my turn. I swallowed hard and began heading toward the direction of the flashing light. As soon as it flashed, we all flattened ourselves against the ground. Slowly, in this manner, we made our way toward the castle porch. Soon, much to my surprise, I felt myself bump into the cement porch. This porch was only about twelve inches high. I raised my head to the top of the porch just as another flash made me duck back down! My heart was pounding madly.

It was then that Fred, the brave one, began the advance. Upon climbing onto the porch, he stood up and swung his pistol at the light.

Crash! The light bulb fell to the ground!

I heard Fred yell, "Damn, it's just the porch light. Someone must have unscrewed the bulb instead of turning the light switch off." We all started laughing uproariously at the debacle, but, also, feeling very relieved at the humorous turn of events. We agreed that the flashing light had to have been activated by the strong gusts of wind.

Soon after, the Navy took over all of the operations, much to our relief.

WHAT ARE YOU DOING
FOR THE WAR EFFORT?

ATTU, 1943

G AS WAS RATIONED; it was wartime in Seattle. Most of us traveled by bus or trolley. People stared at me. It was easy to
read their expressions and the looks in their eyes. "Why
aren't you out there defending our country like my son or
like my husband?"

I didn't feel guilty, but I, too, wondered if I was doing my best. My
draft board had given me a "4-F." They told me that they would not
permit me to be in any military service because of my injuries from the
fall down the mineshaft. I had another medical check late in the fall of
1942 hoping to pass. It appeared that I had passed the check until the
doctor saw the scar on my forehead. He had me stand up and do a
quick touch of the toes ten times. I failed on the second bend-over. I
didn't fall down but I certainly did stagger around to keep from falling.
The doctor was angry. He gave me a big lecture about the danger that I
might have caused in a military situation if I had slipped past his physi-
cal exam.

"I am going to personally write your draft board and make sure that
you do not sneak into some branch of the service."

I couldn't pin a message on my chest explaining my situation nor
could I avoid their thoughts. We were living in Seattle. I had a

worthwhile job as a superintendent of Pier 36 on the Seattle waterfront working for the Army Transportation Corps. We were loading and unloading military cargo every day. Often troops sailed from Pier 36. My boss wasn't going any place because his boss was a full colonel in the Army. I was frozen in my job. The only way out was to be in a combat zone. But I didn't know how to get into a combat zone without being in the service.

I don't recall how I heard about the Army's need for powder experts and rock-drilling specialists in Attu, Alaska. Looking back, I am amazed that I chose to leave my wife, Ann, and my daughter, Janis, to apply for a stint in the Aleutians. But the pressure of the question, "What are you doing for the war effort?" must have been very heavy. In a short time, I walked up the gangplank of a troop ship and was on my way to the farthest-west island in the Aleutian Chain where the Japanese Army was entrenched. I was in the Aleutians for one year. With nothing to do other than work, we worked ten to twelve hour days, taking only Christmas off.

Our ship headed straight across the North Pacific to Dutch Harbor. Dutch Harbor had a large naval base and was the first location to be attacked by the Japanese forces. Much to my surprise we were a single ship operation. No convoy, it was just us out there in the middle of thousands of miles. However, after leaving Dutch one afternoon, the ship's address system came on, saying, "We have just learned that an American vessel has been torpedoed to the west of us. You are to go below, gather up your warm clothing, life jacket, and remain on deck until advised."

Wow! We didn't have any lifeboats but we did have many inflatable rafts hanging in the ship's gear. We were further instructed to be prepared to jump into the water before boarding any of the rafts and to remember to hold down the top of the life vest before you hit the water in case it might strike you in the neck/chin area very hard. With all of these instructions in mind, we spent a very long, cold, rainy, and windy night on deck. All night long we discussed what we would do if our ship was struck. We all agreed that we would not jump into that frozen water and swim to the raft and sit out there in our wet clothing. Instead, we'd go aft on our ship and let what may happen, happen.

The next morning we passed a vessel heading in the opposite direction. It was half of a ship! It was the one that had been torpedoed. It looked so odd steaming along with the front half missing.

One of the wisest decisions I had made on the day of departure was to climb up in the *tween* deck of the number three hatch to the fifth top bunk. Most of the fellows hurried and fought to get a lower berth. We had three big-time storms with 90 percent of the men seasick. I didn't get sick and no one got sick on me. We docked at Adak long enough to take off one man who hadn't eaten in days. We gave him a cheer. He yelled to us, "Fellows, this will be my home until they fly me back to the States."

Late one night I heard and felt the ship's engine slow down. I wondered why. I knew the ship always had a lookout on the bow. I went up on deck, and in the dark I found him.

"What's going on?" I asked.

"Well," the sailor said, "we were entering Massacre Bay here at Attu when suddenly the ship ran into something that slowed our speed. The ship went full-astern. I just found out that we ran into a submarine net. This net keeps the Japanese submarines from coming into the Bay."

The next morning we all went ashore. I recall that on the day we arrived it had only been one or two days since the last big battle on Attu. Later that day I climbed to the area where hundreds of Japanese soldiers lay dead. Many of the fellows went through the dead, looking for souvenirs. Not me. I thought how sad it was. These men were forced to come here and they died for their Emperor.

Theater-made souvenir knife made from aircraft aluminum skin in the Aleutians in 1943.

133

I returned to my designated tent where I met up with the rest of my gang. We were told that we would be taken to our work project in the morning. The colonel in charge of our operation gave us a rundown of what we were to do. He told us that our jobs were very important to the war effort. The Colonel explained the situation this way, "The Japanese have built a landing field for their zeros. Our troops have improved it. However, there are no roads or access to the air field except by barges. You can imagine that this is not very efficient, considering that barges cannot move unless the tides, wind, and weather are favorable. When the barges can get in, the barrels of gas and oil have to be dropped into the water off Alexie Point. Then, men in wet suits 'bull' the barrels ashore. This is where you come in. We need a road and we cannot build it without your help. At this very moment, Kiska Island has been captured by the enemy and our airfield on Attu is the only airport left. We need this road to be punched through as soon as possible."

Now I knew why I was here. It felt good to be part of the war effort, at last.

My tent for the night was pitched on a sidehill. We did have cots and a slim sleeping bag. With the constant rain that night and the pitch of the tent, there was a nice-sized flow of water running through my tent. By morning my socks and packs were soaked.

Our crew consisted of two wagon drill operators, a bulldoze operator, an air compressor engineer, four helpers, and a cook. Don and I were the drillers. The colonel supplied the rest of our gear, including two tents, kitchen stuff, and six soldier helpers to set up camp.

Much to our surprise, we couldn't drive in the tent stakes. The flat beach was solid rock. We fired up the air compressor and drilled holes for iron tent spikes. A cook tent and our sleeping tent was our camp, a hundred yards from the first rock face to be drilled and blasted. I had never seen a wagon drill before. In the mine we had linners. A wagon drill looked just like a linner but was mounted on a three-wheeled rig and was possibly eight times bigger. A linner could drill a 7-foot hole while our monster could drill a 20-foot hole. The Attu rock was not as hard as the Juneau rock, which made it easier and faster to drill and blast. The bulldozer pushed the blasted rock right into the ocean and we then proceeded to drill a new face.

One day when I was idle, due to the bulldozer needing to clear a big pile of blasted rock, I went on an errand to the main encampment. If you were not in your regular area during mealtime, it was proper to stop in at the closest mess tent to be fed.

Before I continue, I must digress to recent history. Possibly two years before World War II broke out, our military started up the Alaska Guard. Major Marvin Marston — whom I later knew when I was on the General Staff—signed up more than 600 Aleuts to watch, protect, and advise of any enemy actions. This was a good idea. Marston did such a good job and was so well liked by the native people that he was called *Muktuk*. Muktuk is the Eskimo name for whale blubber. When the Alaska Guard was brought into the Attu battle, the tides were turned in our favor in no time at all. When it was learned that a few of the Japanese had survived and had taken American uniforms off of American dead, the Army tried to round up all of the Aleuts/Eskimo men as fast as possible to prevent them from being killed as Japanese.

I was glad that there was a handy mess tent because I was good and hungry. I immediately got into line to be served. Much to my surprise, one of the Aleut guardsmen was right in front of me in line. Being a chatty sort and knowing that these men might feel out of place with a different group of soldiers, I tapped him on the shoulder and said, "Hey, soldier, its good to see you. What is the name of your village?"

He turned and gave me an odd stare. The expression on his face seemed to say, "Who are you to be tapping me on the shoulder?"

At that moment I noticed that he glanced up and saw two big MPs enter the tent. He took off on a run. One of the MPs tackled him. My gosh, I thought. He was a Japanese. I had touched the enemy.

I don't recall when we finished the road to the airfield. Our rock road was about four miles long. We finished it before the first snow. The colonel made a special trip to thank us for completing "a job that their engineers could not do. Thank you, men, for a job hastily done."

I thought if the people back home could see me now, I had contributed my best — ten hours a day, seven days a week — for a year.

Ravens on Attu

Attu, 1943

I SPENT a year on Attu, Alaska, during World War II. Attu is treeless. There are bushes and willows, but nothing of any height or stability for perching. Shortly after the island was secured, the Signal Corps installed short poles and strung telephone wires.

It was possibly two or three months after these wires were installed that I saw four or five ravens play a new game. Prior to the installation of the communications wires, living was fairly primitive. There was a small radio shack in the village across the island from Massacre Bay. But if they did have a couple of poles and an antenna, it would have only been there less than five years. It seemed to me that the ravens I observed used original thought, not experiences passed down through the centuries.

One day while I was traveling from my camp to the main camp up in the valley, I became aware of a number of ravens making a lot of noise and circling in the sky. One bird broke out of the pack and took a steep dive toward the earth. Much to my surprise, it zoomed under the communication wire and flared up into the wind. With its wings outstretched, it went into a stall. From the stall and using the wind, it gracefully glided backward down onto the wire. A second raven, timing it perfectly, went into the same steep dive and up under the wire into a stall. At the split second that the second bird drifted backward on to the wire, the first raven leaped straight up into the wind and flew up into the sky. A third, and then a fourth, and a fifth raven duplicated the same maneuver. And then the first bird came back again. They cawed and continued the game until they tired and flew off to do other things.

On another occasion, I witnessed another game that these same five ravens played. It was a game of chicken. Again, they circled about making a lot of noise. After I saw what they did, I wondered if they weren't getting up their courage and trying to talk each other into flying first. Finally, one of them separated from the circling flock. Much to my amazement it folded one wing against its body while leaving the other wing fully extended. From at least 200 feet, it gyrated to within three or four feet of the ground before it extended the other wing and soared up into the sky, all the while cawing and cawing. One after another, the other ravens repeated the "death" dive until they tired of that game, too.

G. I. FOOD

THE SUBJECT of food supplied the servicemen during World War II is an old one and I'll not dwell on it other than to say that the grub dished out to the troops in the Aleutian Islands wasn't any better. On Kiska, we had the usual SPAM, powdered eggs, powdered potatoes, and powdered milk. In retrospect, one realized that the food was really quite good but terribly monotonous. A good example was the jellies and jams that were supplied. Adak only had raspberry jam and Attu received a shipload of strawberry jam. Kiska, unfortunately received marmalade. I never cared for marmalade and now our only dessert was marmalade.

One day the rumor was out that a huge shipment of canned pineapple had arrived. We immediately started to drool. We began to imagine how we might eat the pineapple. One fellow figured that he would take the crushed pineapple and spread it on his bread, heap it onto his spuds, and smother the powdered scrambled eggs. I had decided that my pineapple was going to be of the sliced variety. However a number of days went by, and yet—no pineapple. So we decided to take the supply system into our own hands.

On a lovely, clear night about 10 P.M., the ten of us hunkered down in the snow and observed the routine of the armed sentinel as he walked his post around the supply area. Our booty was stacked up inside the supply tents that, in turn, were heavily laden with snow. Soon we had the guard's pattern worked out. When he disappeared, ten figures silently drifted across the snow and into the tents. Each of us grabbed a case of pineapple and hurried away. Much to our relief there were no challenges or shots from the guard. We assembled on the road amid a great deal of laughing and horseplay. This was the most excitement we had felt in weeks. As an Acey Wagon went by on its way up the hill, we grabbed our cases of pineapple, climbed on, and rode to the turnoff to our hut.

After stomping off the snow and removing our parkas, it was a great scramble as we tore open our cases. The first can that fell onto the floor brought a cry of surprise and curses. The damned pineapple was really fruit cocktail! This fruit cocktail was the kind with the very sweet, sugary syrup. After the initial shock and disappointment of not getting pineapple, we realized it had been only a rumor and that we were lucky the cases weren't full of SPAM or powdered eggs. We regrouped and proceeded to enjoy our new treasures. Three cans of fruit cocktail was all that I could eat before crawling into the sack. The next morning we didn't bother with breakfast except for coffee. We ate fruit cocktail. The noon meal was eaten in the usual manner; however, we rushed over to the hut and had our own private dessert. So it went until we couldn't stand the sight or taste of that horrid stuff. All of the fruit began to taste the same. The pretty red cherries tasted like sweet syrup. The lovely pear chunks tasted just like the pretty red cherries.

Our chow line was formed for every meal immediately outside the side door of the messhall. Waiting for G.I. food in the middle of a snowstorm did not stand out as the best part of one's day, but one evening a thrill of conversation spread down the waiting chow line.

"Wait until you see what we have to eat tonight."

"What is it?"

"Hey, what the hell is it?"

"All I know is that somebody passed the word down."

"Maybe it's turkey or chicken."

Someone else suggested, "How about some pie? How about some pie with a nice thick slice of cheese on top?"

"Yeah! With ice cream, too."

Believe me, we were a group of men looking forward to a special meal!

When I finally got inside the messhall and banged the snow out of my mess kit, I passed on the spuds and SPAM because I was saving space for the good stuff. You could hear the guys yelling, laughing, and saying, "Give me some more!"

"Can we all have seconds?"

"Is there going to be enough to go around?"

When my turn came, cripes! There was the damned fruit cocktail!

"No thanks," I said, "I'll pass."

"Hey!" the K.P. said, "he doesn't want any dessert. Can you imagine not wanting any dessert?"

The fellows just could not understand what was wrong with me. What really hurt was that they served the fruit cocktail every night from then on.

Much later, when the ten of us got back to Attu, we certainly did enjoy eating the lovely strawberry jam. The regulars on Attu couldn't understand how we could eat the stuff.

We could. We'd take strawberry jam, anytime.

Man Overboard!

Seward, Alaska 1945

I WAS WALKING forward to number two hatch when I heard the hatch tender at number one yelling that frightful phrase. "Man overboard!" That cry ran a chill through me.

It was a dark, cold night in early November. The *S.S. Alaska*, a passenger/freighter, arrived at 7 P.M. The passengers remained aboard that night awaiting the departure of the train to the interior in the morning while the longshoremen continued to unload the freight from the ship.

I rushed to the offshore side of the bow where a knot of men had already gathered looking over the side. The reflected light off the dock picked up a fully-clothed man swimming a good, strong stroke around the bow toward the dock. We pushed, shoved, and stumbled over to the other side of the ship to try to keep an eye on this guy. One strange thing that we noted was that he hadn't called for help. That seemed peculiar.

The mate set his crew to breasting the ship away from the dock so that a rescue could be effected. The plan was to send a line down to the man, and if he could not tie himself into the sling, a sailor would go down to aid him.

The hatch tender at number two came up to me and said, "Jeff, this is crazy. That guy came up to me and said, 'I've a good mind to dive down into this hold.' Since he was pretty drunk, I told him to jump down into some other hatch. So he said, 'Okay!' and ran up the deck and dove headfirst into number one hatch. Lucky for him, the hatch had been full up to the hatch-board, so he landed in a nice soft bed of mail sacks. I could hear the longshoremen telling him to get the hell out of the hold and for him to not jump in again. I walked up to see what was going on, and just then he took a big run and dove over the side. I tell you, Jeff, it's crazy."

By this time, the bow had been breasted out, and a sailor was being lowered in a sling. Upon seeing the sailor lowered down to him, the swimmer let go of the piling and swam back under the dock. The bull-rail of the dock as well as the railing of the ship had filled with workers and passengers. Everyone was concerned for his safety, yet confused as to his actions. Many had their own ideas about what should be done and yelled comments and instructions.

"The poor fellow will die of exposure. After all, a person can only survive in this water for twenty minutes."

Another person added, "I think it's only fifteen minutes."

Someone else countered, "Lower a life boat."

"Call the Fire Department."

"Oh, the poor man."

In the meantime, Emil Nelson, one of the dock foremen, accompanied by three men, climbed down through a trap door in the dock and worked their way along the narrow decking installed above high tide. With strong torches they were able to locate the man in the water. Their arrival under the dock coincided with the arrival of Dan Bedford and two men in a skiff that had been launched off the beach. Emil directed Dan toward which bent of piling he should bring his skiff in order to rescue the man. Imagine their surprise when the man swam away from them over into another row of piling. We could hear Dan's exasperated exclamation, "He keeps swimming out of our reach."

Someone on the ship yelled, "Hit the son-of-a-bitch over the head with an oar."

I was amazed at how fast the mood of the crowd changed. Next, I heard someone yell, "Let him drown if he wants to."

At long last, Dan and his men snagged his clothing with an 18-foot boat hook and fought him into their skiff. In the meantime, I had called the ambulance and alerted the hospital. In my telephone conversation the nurse asked me how long the fellow had been in the water.

"Gosh," I replied, "He's still in the water. I think it's been anywhere from thirty-five to forty minutes."

Upon arriving at the hospital, about five men grabbed the rescued swimmer wherever they could and hustled him through the emergency entrance. He was immediately stripped of his clothing and put to bed. The nurses placed many, many hot water bottles along his body and between his legs. Heaps of warm bedding were piled on him. We stepped back wondering if there was anything more we should do.

It was then that I saw a curious thing. The bed was mounted on casters. The bed started to move about the hospital room. Our swimmer was shivering and shaking so much that the bed actually bounced around.

He constantly moaned "I-I-I-M-M-M-C-C-C-O-O-O-L-L-L-D-D-D" over and over. And we all knew that he certainly must have been cold.

Back on the dock, work finally returned to normal. Well actually, it never got back to normal because the men were so completely absorbed in discussing the strange occurrence over and over.

It was much later that I learned that our swimmer had been a war prisoner in a Japanese camp. He had a flashback and thought that he was escaping.

I'm glad that he made it.

THE SCREAMING SWEDE

SEWARD, 1945

H E WAS CALLED "The Swede" or "The Screaming Swede." To his face it was "Hey, Swede!" or just plain "Swede." I never knew him to talk other than in a loud voice; actually, yelling would be more descriptive, as if the wind were blowing or he was in the engine room with two diesels going full blast.

I first saw the Swede in Seward a week after the war was over in 1945. He and a group of soldiers in various stages of military dress, were having a party. The Swede was certainly the loudest, if not the drunkest, of the bunch. You could tell he was a leader of some sort, even though he wore no indication of his rank. He was strictly out of uniform, with a seaman's watch cap, red shirt, Army wool britches, and black fisherman's waders worn at half-mast below the knee. He wore nothing to give away the fact that he actually was in the Army. Swede was an interesting character. I asked about him and this is what I learned.

Fact or fiction, and possibly a part of both, Mr. Johnson's life story ran something like this. I don't recall ever hearing his first name. His father was Swedish, and his mother was an Alaskan Aleut Indian. He was raised in the Alaska Peninsula Aleutian Island/Kodiak area. No doubt the family lived seven months of the year aboard their boat during an extended fishing season. At the age of fourteen years, he shipped out as a deckhand on the mail boat servicing the peninsula and the Aleutian Islands.

Squeaky Anderson of Aleutian Island fame, later admiral and beachmaster of many Pacific Island invasions, was one of his employers. The story has it that on one particular mail delivery, the weather was bad and the seas big. This made it impossible for the mail boat to dock or lay at anchor in order to deliver the mail. The Swede was put over the side in a skiff. With his dory loaded with mail and cargo, he braved the surf and made the deliveries. He was good. He became one of those Alaskans who were wild and woolly but knew the tides and winds and could handle a boat.

The Swede was the skipper on an Army self-propelled barge. A self-propelled bard was the slang for a barge with a house aft that provided quarters for the crew and served as the wheelhouse. Below deck were two diesel engines and auxiliary units. They were twin screw jobs with good maneuverability. There was an anchor forward and two aft. The aft anchors were situated on the two ends of the stern with power winches. For once, the Army used good sense in assigning men to these crafts. Instead of barbers and shoe salesmen, they surprised everyone by crewing them with Alaskan fishermen who were in the service. It was a rough life servicing the little dogholes and outposts in the islands, but these men were born to it and did the job.

On the Swede's vessel, the highest rank was engineer who was a Chief Warrant Officer. The Swede fluctuated from private to sergeant. He was made sergeant and busted so many times that he quit bothering with chevrons. What the heck! He didn't care for rank, anyway. But, he was the captain by virtue of his ability and knowledge. The remainder of the crew was a ragtag bunch of pirates who would make a spit and polish officer go mad. Nonetheless, they got the job done.

In a blinding snowstorm in 1946, about 2 A.M., the Alaska Steamship's freight and passenger ship, the *S.S. Yukon*, ran aground. The location was southeast of Seward on an open, exposed beach. The ship was en route to Valdez, Cordova, and then on south to Seattle. The vessel was driven hard aground, ripping off the bottom aft to the number three hatch. From midship aft, the ship hung off this ledge that was soon to break off, leaving the forward section bouncing up and down in

148

the high seas. Luckily, only twelve people were lost at this time as most of the passengers had been herded forward into the main social hall before the ship broke in half.

There was very little beach backed up by cliffs over 1,000 feet high. Huge seas were running and a number of men were washed overboard and up onto the beach. For a short time a breaches buoy was rigged to the beach, and more men were taken ashore until it became obvious that the soaking wet men on the beach were worse off than those left on the ship. The buoy lines parted, leaving the men stranded without food, dry clothing, blankets, or shelter. The weather was bitterly cold with a wind-chill factor below zero. The Coast Guard, although in charge of the rescue efforts, did not have the proper equipment for a rescue of this type, having only deep-water vessels. They tried to get to the beach with their lifeboats, but the huge rollers breaking onto the rocks made it impossible.

Everyone in this section of Alaska was tuned in to the Coast Guard frequency and followed the fate of the people on the beach. An advisory transmission was made to the Coast Guard headquarters in Kodiak to the effect that rescue efforts had been called off and concern was voiced

The S.S. Yukon *getting hammered on the rocks.*

as to whether the stranded people could survive the night.

This is when the Swede came on the air and said, "Wall, you guys, I tink we'll go in and try to get those poor bastards."

The officer in charge immediately instructed him not to attempt such a dangerous undertaking, finishing with "and this is a direct order."

The Swede came back with, "Wall, I tink we can do it. So, by gosh, that is what we are going to do."

Again, he was given direct orders to turn his vessel out to sea and to keep off the beach. The Swede's response was, "Wall, you can go to hell! And anyway, my radio isn't working anymore and I can't hear anybody."

They called and called but he never came back on the air.

From this account you can tell that he knew what he was doing. It was a well-considered gamble. While still off the beach about a hundred yards, he dropped both stern anchors. With power winches, he slacked off on the anchors as they drove on to the beach. At the same time he kept a tight line, thus preventing the barge from broaching. Should it get broadside in those seas it would surely be lost. Timing the waves, he drove the barge up on the only bit of sandy beach. I wasn't an eyewitness, since I didn't get out there until the following day. But I was told that it was something to see. His crew swarmed ashore. While they were collecting the injured men and preparing to reboard the barge, the Swede reversed his engines and with the help of the two stern anchor windlasses, backed out into deep water. At a signal back on to the beach, he again drove the barge. This time the vessel was further aground making it possible for the men to come ashore over the bow without being swept off by the huge waves. With all aboard, reverse was ordered again. Using his two engines and the stern winches, he crabbed the barge back and forth, twisting and turning. Ahead on one engine, then astern on the other, followed by ahead on the other engine and astern with its mate.

The engineer told me later, "I was running more sand through my engines than water."

Miraculously, back into deep water they did go. By this time both engines had burned out, but they were safe and taken in tow by another boat. The rescued men were transferred to the Coast Guard cutter and raced to the Seward Hospital.

The Army had a difficult time getting the Swede up to Fort

Richardson to accept his medal for heroism. In fact, they put him under protective custody and escorted him to Anchorage. In this way they kept him sober, clean-shaven, and dressed in a proper military manner. He hated wearing a tie worst of all, he told me. But the Army had its way, and Private Johnson was awarded his medal. The troops passed in review. The Swede got roaring drunk that night. Oh, yes! The Army conveniently forgot that he had told the Coast Guard officer in charge to "go to hell."

The Swede took his discharge in Alaska and went back to fishing. His fishing ground was Cook Inlet around Kenai. One night after fishing was over, the Swede anchored at the mouth of the Kenai River. As usual, a number of vessels tied up alongside. During the evening somehow he fell overboard and was swept away with the strong tide. He had never learned to swim. His body was later recovered.

Mr. Ned Skinner of The Alaska Steamship Company, in appreciation for what the Swede did that day on the beach, saw to it that he was properly buried and given a fitting headstone.

The Screaming Swede died like he lived—wild and woolly and one heck of an Alaskan boatman.

THE LAST RUN

WE WERE IN Seattle in 1945. I was the superintendent at Army Pier 36. The war was winding down and with that came the release of manpower that war had required. I could see thousands of men coming home to civilian jobs again and I felt that I should move. Alaska seemed to be calling again. Alaska Steamship Company signed me on to be the assistant agent at Seward, Alaska.

I was received okay at Seward. Very soon it became obvious that my boss had a serious drinking problem, and that I would need to take over the many problems that occurred on a regular basis that he could not handle. I felt lucky that I had worked with the Northland Transportation Company in Sitka and ashore in Seattle with Army Transportation. I did have knowledge and skills that transferred to my new job in Seward. And it became only too clear that I would need to use these skills, plus more, in the coming days. This leads me to "the last run."

On Sunday, February 3, 1946, the *S.S. Yukon* — still under charter from the government — had taken aboard 369 passengers, seventy servicemen, plus the U.S. mail at Seward. I wished Captain Trondsen a good trip and chuckled all the way home at how the *Yukon* still held a special place in my heart ever since it had taken me to Alaska in 1935. My, how that boat had changed my life.

I was home by 11 P.M. The phone rang at 2:30 A.M. It was a newspaper man in San Francisco wanting to check on a report he had received that one of our ships had sent out an S.O.S. He didn't know the ship's name for sure, but he thought that it was the *Yukon*. I told him that I doubted it, because the *Yukon* had just left port about three hours ago. The phone rang again about 5 A.M. It was the Alaska Steamship's operations manager in Seattle advising me of the grounding of the *Yukon*. He further notified me that the Coast Guard had vessels en route from Kodiak and elsewhere. He also told me that he had been trying to get a hold of my boss to no avail.

It was obvious that I needed to step forward and handle as much as I could. I learned that the *Yukon* had run into a blizzard with a strong northeastern wind. Try as he may, Captain Trondsen could not see Erlington Island and finally was swept aground on a narrow beach surrounded by steep cliffs near Cape Fairfield. The weather was still bad but Dr. Bannister, who owned his own airplane, offered to fly me to the area of the grounding. His little plane bounced around a lot, but we did see

Stern view of the Yukon *with the tide in two hours of flood. Note the mast and boom still secured by stays aft of the break.*

the *Yukon's* bow grounded on the beach with only half of the ship left.

I don't recall when the first survivors arrived in Seward, but I think it was about 9 P.M. Joe Grandquist, purser aboard the *Yukon*, was one of the first ashore. Joe wisely carried the passenger list with him. This list would help us keep an accurate count of returning passengers and crew. We learned that the Coast Guard cutter had arrived around noon and had gathered up some passengers. Some of these passengers had been put into a whaleboat and others into a lifeboat. But before the whaleboat could return to rescue others, huge seas broke away the stern leaving all of the remaining passengers in the forward social hall. I figured that Dr. Bannister and I must have arrived right after the stern broke away. I learned further that at some point in the afternoon, big forty-foot waves carried twenty-one men over the side. Some were rescued by an Army barge, some made it ashore, and some were carried back on board. The Navy attempted a rescue, too, but found the waves too large to perform their maneuvers. I was told that the Coast Guard at one point ran a

Bow view of the Yukon *with the tide flooding for five hours. Note the large boulders on the beach.*

shallow draft boat in close to the *Yukon*. They saw at a glance that it was impossible to come alongside it, so they anchored their craft a safe distance from the *Yukon* and got a line aboard. Then they used a raft and ferried the people from the *Yukon* to the Coast Guard boat.

The mate told me, "It wasn't easy to get people into the raft. One moment the raft would be even with the Yukon's deck, and the next moment it would be at least eight feet lower. Until the Coast Guard got the timing down, they dumped a few men into the water." A line had been tied around each person's waist for easy retrieval. However, nothing was easy in that storm. The Coast Guard had many smaller boats ready to help. These boats took the rescued people into Seward.

This is where I came in. I personally checked off each passenger or crew member's name as they slowly arrived. The Seward General Hospital was a small one and not able to handle the number of cold, wet people. Immediately, the people of Seward opened up their homes to take in whoever did not have a bed. This went on all night until possibly noon the next day. Prior to my going to bed that night, I learned that I would be in charge of a special boat departing at 7 A.M. the next morning for the *Yukon*. I would be accompanied by eight to ten of the Army's Alaska Scouts plus the postal inspector. Rumors ran high that bodies were left aboard and hope was to get a party aboard before the big waves took the last half of the ship off the shelf to be lost forever. The post office was sending a postal inspector to check the mail on board and especially the gold in the mail shipment. At that time, gold was shipped via the U.S. mail and often placed in special, small, stout mail sacks. Each sack had a leather riveted top and a metal strap with a padlock.

We departed right at 0700 hours on a regular Coast Guard boat. The sea was calm and it was clear and sunny. Upon arriving in the area, we ended up using a self-propelled barge to come alongside the Yukon. The surf was down but it was still tricky to get aboard. One of the most important objectives of this mission was to locate and bring back any victims or bodies.

The first mate told me, "There is a dead man in my cabin. While attempting to get into a rescue raft, he fell and died of a possible head injury. We felt the best temporary thing to do was to carry and place this body in my room, away from the turmoil."

156

While the scouts scoured the remaining ship for any life or more bodies, I dragged the dead man out of the first mate's cabin and down to the main deck where we placed him on the barge. We then proceeded to look for the gold that was being transported. The postal inspector and I, using a sounding line, tested the depth of the number three hatch where the gold was stowed. We found that the bottom of the ship had been sheared off a few feet below the *tween* deck. The force of the waves had blown off the hatch covers and everything in the holds was lost.

Later, we went ashore in the barge and checked items that had washed up on the beach. A number of the gold pouches were there with the bottom of the pouches blown open and the gold lost in the surf. Before completing our mission, I went up to the bridge. I gathered up some loose papers, the logbook, and bid farewell to the *S.S. Yukon*. It was gone after the next storm.

OLD LADY LECHNER

SEWARD, 1947

"M R. JEFFREY, I want to see you right away."

That was Mrs. Lechner on the phone. I just hated those calls. She didn't ask if you could find time, or when would you be available, or if you were coming past the office — could you please stop in? Oh no, it was always, I want to see you right away. And you saw her right away; except, of course, if you were rushed to the hospital because a heart attack. Come to think of it, it was always a good idea to stop by, or you would be sorry.

The Lechners were old-timers in Seward. Mr. Lechner, or Charlie as we all called him, arrived in Seward from Germany around 1914, settled himself, got a job, and then sent for Margaret. The two were married the day her ship arrived. They had a son, young Charlie, who came along much later, possibly not until 1921. The two Charlies ran the Seward Machine Shop. During the World War II, they made lots of money having a complete machine shop, and Uncle Sam was their best customer. Charlie Sr. sure was a nice old guy.

Mrs. Lechner found out real fast that her husband was a good shopman, but a poor businessman. She took over the business end. Mrs. Lechner was sharp and definitely knew the business. And nobody ever got the best of her! As a side business, they also operated the Ford Agency and sold washing machines and refrigerators.

All three — the business, the shop, and the home — were run by Mrs. Lechner. The men folk had long since stopped having ideas or making suggestions. Being an old-timer gave her the *whiskers* to know how the city was run years ago, at the present, and how it should be run in the future. She was all-knowing, all-seeing, and all-smelling. And, you'd better not forget it! Her pen was mightier than her phone calls. She penned letters to my boss, the mayor, the governor, Alaska's representative to Congress, and if she didn't get her way, she went straight to the head guy — the President! Do you think I am kidding? Well, I am not.

I suppose she was fifty-five years old in 1947, when I received her summons. She looked older, but I am trying to be kind. She was short and skinny. Her washed-out blue eyes and a ping-pong-ball-sized nose in a wrinkled face didn't add anything to her beauty. Her hair was thin. You could see the scalp through the short, tight curls she always wore. I never saw her smile. You might have called the straight line of thin lips a smile when something went her way. I almost forgot one other thing, and then we'll return to the phone call: If she was not winning a point or getting her way, she would grasp her left breast, and in a faint voice say, "My angina." With that, we would back off. After all, you didn't want to be the one to send her to her grave.

She ruled her menfolk this way, too. One day I was driving out the road and saw the two Charlies in their car alongside the road. I stopped and inquired, "Hey, what are you guys doing?"

Charlie Sr. said, "Mother decided it was time for the two of us to get away from work and go have some fun. We had work to do and didn't want to play. But, her angina started acting up, so here we are. We don't know what the hell we are supposed to do to have all that fun."

This was an extra busy day. Christmas was a few days off. The *S.S. Denali* as well as the *M.V. Susitna*, were in port. The boat train was to be in at 7:30 P.M. It was almost dinnertime at the hospital and I always made it a point to be there and help Janis with her evening meal. Janis, our six-year-old daughter, had been hospitalized and extremely ill throughout the fall with meningitis. As of December, the hospital staff assured us that Janis would live, but could not promise that she would ever walk again.

"Dammit," I muttered. "Mrs. Lechner knows my schedule — and

almost everyone else's schedule in town. She knows that this is a super-busy day. Why in the hell doesn't she consider other people for a change?"

It was a short walk to her office, but I prepared a number of speeches I knew I would never give, telling the old girl where to go.

With a forced smile on my face, I opened the door to her tiny office. She looked up and said, "Oh, Jack, I am glad you could come over right away." She called me Jack.

Hmm, I thought. It was Mr. Jeffrey on business, and Jack if it was personal.

"I have a little package here for Janis. I was so worried it wouldn't get here before Christmas. I ordered it plenty early from Switzerland, but it didn't come, and it didn't come. But, now it is here. It is a music box. I hope it will fill some of her slow times in the hospital with happy music. Now, run along, because I know this is a very busy day for you."

I was crushed! I must have mumbled some sort of a thank you to her. I hurried out into the dark to hide the tears forming in my eyes. What terrible thoughts I had concocted about Mrs. Lechner. I felt like I should return and apologize.

With great glee, Janis opened the box. She played the music over and over. It was such a wonderful present. We made it a practice to turn

Janis in the hospital.

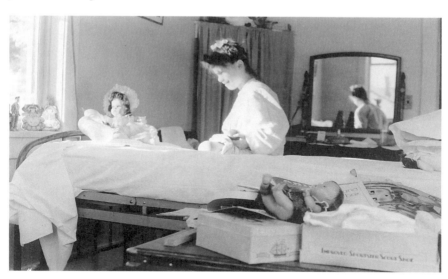

it on every night, prior to my departure. I could hear the music follow me down the hall as I left. The nurses told me the other patients listened for the music which told them all was well, and Janis was settled for the night.

Mrs. Lechner did have a heart problem. All of that time we thought she was bluffing. She's gone now. Nevertheless, wherever you are, Mrs. Lechner — I apologize.

FLYING IN ALASKA

BUSH FLYING — "HOURS OF MONOTONY AND SECONDS OF SHEER TERROR"
LATE '40s TO LATE '50s

CHRISTIANSON AIR SERVICE flew between Anchorage and Seward carrying mail, freight, and passengers in the late 1940s. As a rule, it was one flight a day. Arrival in Seward was set for 10 A.M., subject to weather and the ever-present low ceiling. During the winter it was common to not have a flight for three to seven days, despite the desire of the airline to get in and make a buck.

The plane they used the winter day that I flew north with them was a Travel Air on wheels. It was a slow, heavily loaded plane when we took off. As a rule, I moved pretty fast when it was passenger loading time and in that manner—more often than not—sat in front in the right-hand seat. It was cold and windy but clear. After we got aloft, the pilot trimmed his controls, eased back on the throttle, and set the mixture and spark. There was a great deal of vibration noise. Due to this vibration, I suppose, the pilot locked his throttle settings with one of the largest clothespins that I have ever seen. But it did the job—holding the throttle and the other two levers in place. In no time, it was noticeable how heavy the plane was because it was sinking at the normal cruise setting. This was corrected, but I remember thinking, "This baby must have the glide of a dead duck without power."

The flight was a joy until we approached Turnagain Arm. As you possibly know, during the winter Turnagain Arm and Cook Inlet are just a jumble of turning, grinding ice. The big tides prevent the water from freezing up, thus the huge ice cakes and sheets of ice. Tom Maloney's son, while on a student flight, had gone down into the inlet just nine days previous. He didn't have a chance. In fact to my knowledge, no flyer down in the arm or the inlet during the winter months ever survived. I tried to keep these thoughts at rest, but my heartbeat quickened and I knew that I would be relieved when we reached the other shore.

About a third of the way across, as the pilot was broadcasting to the field, the roar of the engine dropped to a murmur and the propeller began idling. Immediately the plane started a steep descent, and I doubt that we were over 1,000 feet at the time. Our glide path pointed to about 300 yards offshore. The pilot quickly switched tanks and hastily checked other things to correct our problem. In a panic I looked around and thought, Gosh! What can I do? What can I do?

Suddenly I zeroed in on the throttle. The clothespin had vibrated off and the throttle had retarded itself. The engine had not stopped but was slowly idling. Immediately and without thinking I pushed the throttle to full. The engine took and we were flying again.

The pilot yelled at me over the noise of the motor, "You're not supposed to do that! I am the pilot!" He was very upset and I knew his yelling at me was just a natural reaction.

That moment of terror was past and we went on into Merrill Field without incident.

Christianson Air Service purchased a new plane. It was the exact same model that President Eisenhower used to move about the country on short hops. I think that it was called an Aero Commander. It was a neat plane and I looked forward to flying in it.

It was a chilly day so the passengers were crowded into the small office waiting room until boarding time was announced. Prior to boarding, I asked Chris if I could sit up front in his nice new plane. In turn, he asked me if I would do him a favor and not ride in the Commander since a large group had already filled the plane.

"I'm taking the Waco this trip," Chris said, "and if you ride with me, we'll look for game."

That cinched it for me. The Waco was a biplane with lots of power and a plane that Chris preferred to fly especially if the flying conditions were a little iffy.

We had a big load of mail and air freight as Chris and I took off ahead of the Commander. The trip was fun. We took the long way to Seward flying down valleys and alongside mountains. We saw lots of moose, goats, and sheep. With all of that power in the biplane, Chris flew plenty close to the game and mountains. Since we had taken an unusual length of time in our flight to Seward, we were surprised that the Commander had not arrived ahead of us. Oh, well. Maybe they had a delay departing Anchorage, we thought.

I didn't hear until that afternoon that the Aero Commander had crashed on a mountainside near Skilak Lake. There were no survivors.

A lady and I were the only passengers on this beautiful day from Anchorage to Seward. I don't recall the exact type of plane other than it carried the pilot, one passenger in front and a backseat for three.

Today, they piled mail into the backseat behind the pilot and on the floor, leaving room for me behind the lady. As I strapped myself in, I noticed and remarked to the pilot that the mail wasn't tied down in any manner. He replied with a wave of the hand and a shrug indicating that it wasn't necessary. Okay, I thought, he's the professional.

Being a perfect day with unlimited visibility, we went right up and leveled off above the highest mountain. Our flight was straight as an arrow. The usual winding down canyons and keeping under the ceiling or maintaining visual contact with the ground was not necessary today. It was beautiful. As you possibly know, these pilots always had the following in mind: save gas and keep the flight as short as possible. As a result, one moment you might be 3,000 feet in the air, and the next you felt like holding your feet up as you skimmed over a mountain-top followed by being 3,000 feet high again.

After crossing Turnagain Arm, we picked up Hope and the highway. On down the road you could see where it branched out. One road led to Coopers Landing and Kenai and the other road led to the east to Moose Pass and Seward. We were high and continued to fly straight ahead. Soon we were over Crescent Lake, which is a beautiful body of water high up in the Alpine tree zone. The mountain sheep, as a rule, are below the lake. We figuratively held up our feet as we skimmed over the lake, for I knew that once clear of the lake, the mountain dropped off thousands of feet to Kenai Lake below.

Suddenly we were caught in the most violent turbulence that I have ever experienced in a small plane, followed by a maximum downdraft. The pilot and his passengers were strapped in their seats but the mail was floating in the air. Down we went and I have no idea how far. Our downward motion quickly stopped, and a good majority of the mail came down upon the pilot knocking him forward against the

Float plane on the beach.

166

instrument panel. The pilot's position pushed the yoke forward and had us in a steep dive. We were really moving straight at the lake at a high rate of speed. I tore off my seatbelt and in a panic, heaved mail sacks off the pilot. I was relieved to see movement under the sacks so I knew that he was conscious. A few more sacks and he came up from under the pile. Two more sacks were yanked out from behind his back and he was able to sit erect and pull the yoke, stopping our plunge toward the lake. Our margin of escape was far too close.

The next day during coffee break on the dock, I overheard two longshoremen talking about a sight that they had seen the day before. They had been at mile twenty-four near the Forest Service buildings and had seen a plane diving toward the lake.

"It looked like they were playing chicken," one said, and believe me they almost lost! It was far too close to the lake before they pulled up." I agreed.

Cordova Airlines had recently purchased Christianson Air Service when I took the return trip to Seward after doing business in Whittier. We were flying in a DC-3, one of the best airplanes ever constructed. They could pack a good payload in comfort and had fuel enough for eight hours.

It was a dark and overcast day. Word had been received that there was minimum ceiling in Resurrection Canyon, so the flight could be made. To understand the problem, it is necessary to draw a rough mental sketch of the canyon and explain the course the plane had to take. With good visibility the planes flew high enough to proceed straight down the canyon and above the obstruction that would be called a butte in Montana, a hill in Washington, or a mountain in Florida. You name it. Whatever that mound can be called, it's a crucial factor in this story.

Prior to departure from Anchorage, the owner of Cordova Airlines and an old-time bush pilot, Merle "Mudhole" Smith, came aboard and went forward into the pilot's compartment. In an informal manner, the door was left open for all to see the activities up front. Upon getting squared away after takeoff, the pilot turned the controls over to the co-pilot and he and Smith had a great gab-fest. They must have been regaling each other with their many experiences for there was a great deal of laughter.

Until high-flying jets came into the business, I always looked down at the countryside. On bush flights, I most often knew where I was and what was coming up next. I was on the starboard side watching things when I saw the mound appear up ahead. The pilot started the normal turn to the right to avoid the mound. He kept on turning, and turning, and turning. Suddenly it dawned on me that the co-pilot was heading up the dead-end box canyon. I ripped loose my seat belt and ran up the aisle yelling, "You're going up the wrong canyon! Turn left! Turn left!"

The captain swung around, took one look, and took over the controls. He poured on the power and went into a steep, banking turn. We made it by the skin of our teeth.

They shut the door and remained in there until I debarked. No doubt they were ashamed of themselves and terribly embarrassed. I wonder how many airplane accidents could have been avoided if they would have had passenger participation?

A Christmas Story

THE *S.S. ALASKA* was in port and Christmas would arrive in just a few days. I remember that particular Christmas being miserably cold and snowing hard. I think it was 1951. My job was moving freight and passengers in the seaport of Seward, Alaska, for The Alaska Steamship Company. There were many things that needed attention with this job, so it was with some irritation that I looked up at Mary's interruption.

"Jeff, there's a nice little old lady out here who that says she wants to see you. I tried to talk to her, but she insists that she must see you. Will you come out and talk to her, please?"

My *customer* was about five feet tall, in her seventies, very thin, and obviously very upset. I asked what I could do for her, and she replied, "I was sent to you. I am without funds. I have also been evicted from my room. I was sent to you for help."

Gosh, I thought. What a dirty trick for someone to sick this old gal on me. What can I possibly do? Obviously, she was in desperate need, but where could she go for help? The least that I could do was to listen to her story.

She told me something about herself. She had no family, and a succession of menial type jobs over the past years had left her penniless.

Among the many places that she had worked, she mentioned the orphanage in Valdez. As she explained it, "They told me that if I ever wanted to work there again, that they would be pleased to reemploy me."

This seemed like a possible lead, but, after all, that was some time ago. Circumstances change, and she was in Seward, not Valdez. I suddenly hit upon a possible solution and asked her, "Would you like to go to Valdez and work in the home?"

Her reply was quick. "Oh, yes! I'd dearly love that."

So I told her to sit down and take it easy and that I would see what could be done. We had a teletype hookup with Valdez, so I punched out a message to the company agent:

"Hey, John, I've got a little old lady here by the name of Ethel Swanson who claims that she worked at the children's home there in Valdez. She's broke and needs a job, not to mention a roof over her head. How about checking with the home?"

In a matter of minutes, the teletype clattered back, "She's hired! Send her on the *Alaska*. The home is picking up the tab for a minimum room. Debit my office."

Armed with this good news, I prepared her ticket and called her to the counter. She moved slowly toward me with that lost look still on her face, not knowing what to expect. I explained the situation to her and handed her a ticket.

"Here is your ticket to Valdez. The ship leaves tonight. You have a job at the children's home you mentioned to me earlier. Normal boarding time is after dinner; however, it will be arranged for you to go aboard immediately. Plan on having lunch and dinner on the ship, and your stateroom will be open — so feel free to use it. A nice long nap after lunch might be a good idea. You see, things aren't really that bad, and everything has worked out okay."

While I spoke, her arms rested on the counter and she leaned forward listening intently. Much to my discomfort, she suddenly started to cry — no sobs, no noise — just tears that cascaded down her cheeks, and splashed off the counter. She began to tell me a story.

"This morning, I was at the end of my rope. I haven't eaten since yesterday's breakfast. When the landlord told me that I had to leave, I just didn't know what to do. In desperation, I got down on my knees, and prayed to God. I told him my problems and the things I had tried to do to help myself. And I asked Him, 'What should I do now? To whom can I turn?' Suddenly, somehow, I knew what to do. My prayer was answered and the Lord sent me to you. You have taken care of everything. I'll have a job; my room and meals will be furnished; and, best of all, I'll be with friends at Christmas. Yes, the Lord, truly, answered my prayers."

Still silently crying, she gave me a long look and with a grand gesture toward heaven, said, "You, sir, are the instrument of the Lord."

By this time, the pool of tears had enlarged beyond belief, and I turned to Mary and Irene for help. Surely, they could get me out of this uncomfortable situation. But, they sat stiff in their chairs, listening to every word and nodding in agreement, tears streaming down their faces.

"Come on," I pleaded, "will you finish taking care of Mrs. Swanson? I have work to do." And with that, I hurried out the door.

As I headed for the dock, I noticed that it had stopped snowing and the sky had cleared. Everything was covered with fluffy white flakes and the harbor was a brilliant blue jewel in a setting of sheer white mountains. What did it matter that work would be slowed while the snow was cleared away? It was beautiful!

As I boarded the ship, I thought that there are deluxe rooms empty at this time of year. Why not berth Mrs. Swanson in one of those? The steward's department will want to put flowers and candy in her room and serve her breakfast in bed. I found the purser, and had him make the necessary arrangements, laughing to myself as I did so.

"Because when you are the instrument of the Lord, you have to go first class all the way!"

A SEA STORY

THIS SEA STORY is about Captain Percy Selig. Everyone called him "Blackie" and no wonder with a name like Percy. Blackie was the skipper on the passenger ship *S.S. Alaska* for years. During this period, about the 1950s, he was at the height of his glory. There were men passengers to shoot the bull with, and ladies, young and old, with whom to flirt!

Captains on big ships do not stand at watch. Every member of the crew stands at watch and is busy, whereas the captain has nothing to do except oversee when everything is going along normally. At other times he is on deck for whatever length of time it takes to return to normal. So it was a real blow to Blackie when the Alaska Steamship Company went out of the passenger business and only hauled freight.

The *S.S. Iliamna* was his freighter — or cargo ship — with a crew of twenty-six men. After a number of trips, you have heard every story and every joke from everyone on the ship. Time really drags for the old man, especially if he is active both mentally and physically. As a result, Blackie was into many things. He tried writing. He painted with oils and watercolors, the latter turning out to be one of his better ventures. And his mind was always active.

The *S.S. Iliamna* docked in Seward before breakfast. As usual, I met the boat and got my immediate business taken care of before eating breakfast with the officers. Blackie was just finishing off a can of grape juice when I was called on deck. Upon returning to finish my meal, the skipper had left the galley and the second and third mates were discussing the "grape juice kick" that the old man was on.

"Yeah," the second mate said. "This is the second trip that the old man has been drinking the stuff."

It turns out that he was drinking seven to eight cans every day.

"He looks kind of funny with his tongue colored black all of the time. I don't get it, it seems that he would get tired of the same old stuff, and switch to apple juice or something."

Later, I went up on to the bridge where Blackie was watching the progress of the work on deck. I asked him, "Hey, Blackie! What's the deal with you and the grape juice? It's the talk of the crew."

"Good, good!" he said. "That's what I want. In a day or two I'll let the cat-out-of-the-bag and we'll see if those suckers take the bait." I urged him to tell me his big plan, but no soap! He wouldn't tell.

"Okay!" I said. "Will you promise to tell me the whole story when it breaks?"

He promised.

The freighters made a round-trip every three weeks. I could hardly wait for the return of the *Iliamna*. In the meantime, Ann and I had speculated on the *why's* of the grape juice scenario even to the possibility that Blackie owned stock in the grape juice company.

My routine upon a ship's arrival was to turn the mail and company papers over to the purser and then immediately go over the discharge plans with the first mate. As I talked to these two men I was amazed to see that their tongues were blackish-blue.

Hmm, I thought. Grape juice. At breakfast it appeared that only Blackie was drinking grape juice. Upon completing his meal, the captain said to me, "Jeff, I'd like to see you in my room when you are through."

I finished my toast in short order and climbed the three decks to his room looking forward to the answer of the mystery of the grape juice drink. Blackie unfolded the story like this:

Back three trips prior to arriving in Seattle, I asked the chief steward to make a special order for me. I wanted him to have on hand for every voyage enough grape juice for me to have seven cans of juice every day. I also asked him to instruct the messman to keep at least that amount chilled. He was to be alert and to report to me if any other member of the crew drank grape juice—and I expected those cans to be replaced. Jimmy Thompson, the chief steward, took this request as an order and the stewards took care of the old man. It wasn't long until the crew started to talk it up and even began asking me what the deal was. My reply was always the same, "I just like grape juice a lot."

Well, after talking to you on the last trip I felt that the time was ripe. One evening I relieved the first mate and stood his watch for a couple of hours. Fred, the quartermaster, asked me, "Captain, can I ask you a personal question?"

"Sure!" I said. "You can ask me anything but that doesn't mean that I'll answer you."

"It's all about that grape juice that you have been drinking. What, for God's sakes, is the reason?"

I didn't answer for a while. I looked at him and said, "Can you keep a secret?"

Of course he couldn't. And I also knew that the crew on this ship couldn't keep a secret. So I told him, "I'm not getting any younger. These long trips away from home and the short stay in Seattle places quite a demand on me in bed. You know what I mean?" He said that he understood.

"Well, a guy likes to think that he will perform at least adequately." He also agreed to that. So I told him, "I learned that grape juice does the stuff. It is the ticket. Why, after only one trip of drinking the stuff, I was performing like I was a twenty-year-old. So that is the reason for the grape juice. I really hate the stuff, but it's worth it."

"So, Jeff! You see, the secret really worked! Reports are coming in that it really works. I guess that if you think it will work, it does!"

Blackie went on to other tricks and activities, but for me, that one was the best. Whenever I see a can of grape juice, you can be sure that I think of Blackie!

S. S. Victoria

J. RAMSAUER, *Commander*

Luncheon

Thursday March 7, 1935

Garden Radishes   Spring Onions

Puree Chantilly   Beef Bouillon

Broiled Black Cod   Lemon Butter

Grilled Luncheon Steak   Fried Onions

Steamed Frankfurters and Sauerkraut

Rice Pancakes with Honey

French Carrots   Saute Potatoes

Grilled Breakfast Bacon   Eggs any Style   Broiled Premium Ham

COLD BUFFET

Cold Meats with Potato Salad

Prime Ribs of Beef with Horseradish

Roast Leg of Veal   Kippered Herring   **Bologna Sausage**

Liberty Salad   Cream Dressing

Grape Nut Pudding   Cream Sauce

Loganberry Jello With Whipped Cream

Pumpkin Pie   Lady Cake   Apricot Pie

Preserved Plums

American   Cottage   or   Pimento Cheese

Black and Green Tea

Fresh Milk   Coffee   Buttermilk   Chocolate

ARTHUR PAYNE, *Chief Steward*

A typical menu on an Alaska Steamship Line passenger ship.

BANANAS

THE *M. V. SUSITNA* made fast to the Army Dock in Seward at 0700 hours and went to work at 0800. The Alaska Steamship Company had asked me to be present during the discharge of a special stow of bananas. The entire lower hold of number four hatch had been stowed with bananas. This was the *reefer* hatch that could be used for a cool room or cold storage. In this case, the temperature had been set for 52° to 54° Fahrenheit — the optimum temperature for bananas.

The square — the opening in the lower hold — was small, and with the cargo of bananas stowed head-high, only four men and one cargo-board could be worked at one time. Four sailors climbed down the short ladder to the floored-off cargo. The winch driver lowered a cargo-board to the men who unhooked it and prepared to stow the boxes of bananas on to the board. The captain, first mate, purser, and I were on the main deck leaning against the hatch, looking down into the hold. To our amazement, one of the sailors who had walked back out of the square a short distance, slumped down onto the cargo and stayed there. Another sailor who picked up a case, placed it on the cargo board, and then he, too, lay down on the board. Almost immediately the other two sailors toppled over.

The bosun, who had been standing in the *tween* decks, climbed down the ladder to help his men. He went to the man farthest out in the wings, who had collapsed first, and dragged him to the cargo board. Then, the bosun staggered around and fell onto the board. I recall the first mate yelling, "Get the blowers going. Get a hold of the engine room. Where are the other sailors?"

The winch-driver below yelled, "Lower the slings, so that we can hook up to the board."

Believe me, there was some fast action for a few moments. Luckily, an engineer was standing by and threw the switches to activate the blowers. Four other sailors hurried down the ladder and dragged their buddies onto the cargo-board. Two of these sailors, the first ones down, slumped onto the pile of men while the other two hooked up the board. Nine men were hoisted out of the hold. Once on deck they quickly revived.

What was all of this about? I found out right away. Luck had nothing to do with the engineer being on hand. He was really wound up. The sailors had demanded the blowers be turned off before breakfast to give the hatch a little time to warm up. To top that, they had told the mate that they wouldn't work in the hold with the blowers going at all.

"I told you wise guys we should keep the blowers going to keep the level of carbon dioxide at a low level. But, no! You wouldn't listen!" said the chief engineer.

While in Seattle, I talked to some people who sailed on a banana boat. They told me that you can't last over a minute in a hold with the blowers off. For the rest of the time, believe me, the sailors worked that hatch with the blowers going full-blast!

SLAUGHTER GULCH

IT WAS NEAR THE END of the first moose season and I still hadn't gotten my moose. As a rule, I scored by noon of the first day. You see, what happened was that I had heard of a better way to get our moose.

In the past, we had gone out the road every morning in hopes of tagging one a half-mile off the road. Or, we flew into some lake. We even tried boating on the lakes and rivers. This time, we were about to try a sure-fire, easy way to hunt. We were told, "All the creeks on the Kenai Peninsula have firm gravel beds. All you have to do is to take a four-wheel-drive truck up any of the streams during low water, and it's a piece of cake. Go as far as you want, make camp, and hunt. Load your meat on the truck and drive home."

It sounded great! So, we decided to try this new method.

That's another story. But I will mention that we went too far up the creek, dropped into a hole, and flooded out the engine. That night a huge storm flooded the stream almost to the top of our cab. We escaped with just our rifles and packboards. It was two weeks before we could return to our truck and all of our gear. Talk about being up that prover-bial creek without a paddle! We had had it, but it took us weeks to retrieve everything.

That's why Ann and I had this date to fly in to the lake at Slaughter Gulch. With a name like that, we were a cinch to knock over a moose. Our appointed time was 2 P.M. We were at Jim's cabin on Kenai Lake above Cooper's Landing by 1:30 P.M. Flying hunters in and out, gassing up, and all of that is not an exact science, so we knew 2 P.M. was tentative. By 3 o'clock, we began to worry about getting into our camp before nightfall. Toward the end of September, the darkness always came earlier than we expected. We had eaten breakfast early and then followed it with an early lunch. Looking ahead, I thought that this might be one of the times I should possibly follow my father's admonishment: "When you are away from home and uncertain of the situation, go to the bathroom and eat whenever, you can."

Jack and Ann with some moose meat from "another day."

So I said, "Ann, let's have something to eat in the lodge."

She came back with, "I'm not hungry, but you go ahead, if you want to." And, I did.

Around 4 o'clock, Jim came into the landing. While I helped him gas up, he told me of his problem with the last bunch of hunters that he had flown. We loaded the gear, piled in, and departed. The gulch is right above the lodge on the East side. To get there it was only a matter of circling for altitude and then landing. We made a pass over the lake to see if it was clear to land and to check the wind direction. It's unlawful to hunt from an airplane, but it's not illegal to look out of the plane as you circle and land at your hunting destination.

About a hundred yards from the lake, a big, old moose stood in the willows. We unloaded our gear, bid Jim a hasty goodbye, and went hunting. Luckily, I was smart enough to pocket a flashlight. In no time we were into the thicket and within fifty feet of our quarry. The moose had not moved. I didn't shoot because the willows were so thick and I was sure that my shot would be deflected. A missed shot is okay but a wounded animal was not.

Ann stayed in a vantage spot while I circled around for a better shot. Twice I checked with Ann, and her nod and hand signal indicated that the moose was still in the same spot. The next check Ann gave me was a shake of her head and a shoulder shrug. It had gone. We were amazed that such a huge animal could turn around and melt away without a sound.

Before we got out of the brush, my flashlight had to be used. I should have known better than to just dump all of our gear and head out hunting. The unwritten rule is to always set up your camp first. In haste and in the dark, we pitched our tiny mountain tent in just "any old place" and crawled in out of the bitterly cold wind. Our good sleeping bags were up that stream with the truck at our first camp, as were our food box, gasoline stove, and cooking gear. I climbed into my sack by the light of our flashlights, and said, "Goodnight. Sleep as well as you can with the rocks and uneven ground bothering you all night."

Ann replied, "Goodnight! What do you mean — goodnight? I haven't had anything to eat."

She looked forlorn eating date bread and cheese while sitting half out of her bag. It was with a touch of wisdom that I didn't remind her that she had chosen not to eat at the lodge.

The following day turned out much better. After all, things can't go wrong forever. But, that's another story!

A Holiday Sailing

THE CHRISTMAS SEASON was a popular time for Alaskans to travel and almost all staterooms were booked on the *S.S. Baranof* out of Seward. She was due to sail during the Christmas season at 10 P.M. for the southbound ports of Valdez, Cordova, Juneau, Petersburg, Wrangell, Ketchikan, and Seattle.

As was the custom, a number of Anchorage people had come down on the boat train to see family members or friends off in style. As sailing time approached, I could tell that business in the local bars was thriving and in the local vernacular, "We would be pouring them on the boat!"

Standard procedure, once the sailing time was posted, was to blow the half-hour whistle and then the fifteen-minute whistle. The blast was heard in all staterooms and even uptown in homes and bars. In this way everyone was alerted that departure was imminent.

On this particular night, as he had done for years, the captain came on the public address system approximately seven minutes before departure to announce, "Attention, please. We will be sailing within a few minutes. All passengers ashore."

I heard all of this in the back of my mind and thought, good. We'll get those visitors ashore in good time and sail promptly. I had a few final things to take care of and then stood at the bullrail awaiting the lowering of the gangplank. About then, I tuned in on the exchange between the people lining the ship's rail and those standing on the dock.

"Yah, sure, Fred! I know you hadn't planned on going instead of me. Ha! Ha! I think my clothes will fit you a bit snug. Sure, you can use my toothbrush. Hardy har!"

Other similar exchanges were going on between the thirty or so people on the dock and those on the ship.

What's going on? I wondered. I grabbed the man next to me, who I knew was a southbound passenger, and asked him, "How come you're not aboard?"

His reply was, "Well, hell! The captain told us 'All passengers ashore' didn't he? He's the boss, ain't he? Gotta do what the captain said or they'll call it a mutiny, won't they? Isn't that right, Fred?"

As I replayed the captain's announcement in my mind, I thought, Yep, that's what he said. Oh, my god! As fast as possible, I hurried up the plank, advising the first mate to hold everything. It was with utter disbelief that the captain heard my explanation of the situation.

Shaking his head, he said, "I can't believe it. I just can't believe it."

Then came his second announcement, "Attention, please. Will all visitors go ashore? Will all the passengers on the dock, please, come aboard?"

You can imagine the exchanges between the two groups as they changed places for the departure. As the ship slipped away into the darkness, I said to the dock foreman, "Those guys had a bit too much Christmas cheer."

"Yah," Dan replied, "more like New Year's!"

MARTIN GORESON

SEWARD, 1957

SEWARD, ALASKA, was a one-industry town: transportation. Before people learned to make Anchorage a year-round port, all cargo to the interior of Alaska was transported by ships to Seward. At Seward the cargo was off-loaded and forwarded via the Alaska Railroad. Later, a highway was punched to Anchorage connecting Seward with the network of roads in the interior.

Peak transportation months — May through September — seldom found Seward without a ship in port. Our firm alone, the Alaska Steamship Company, ran two passenger/cargo ships plus one freighter every week. When in port, the ships worked to the capacity of the port and manning ability of the longshoremen unions. If you were a card-carrying longshoreman, you could almost work every day of the month. Our work program consisted of two shifts of ten hours each. Other than early-day mining, longshoring was one of the few types of job that allowed a man to pull the plug — or lay off for a while — and then go right back to work.

This free and easy way of working and not working suited most of the 350 men in this trade. Peak employment hired any warm body. When a vessel only worked three or four hatches, a man could pull his peg, giving work to some other idle man.

Martin Goreson was a longshoreman by choice. He was also a fisherman, a game guide, a carpenter, truck driver, and I suppose he was other things that I didn't know. In the fall, Martin took out big game hunters from the States. In June, he always went to Bristol Bay for the red salmon run. Oh, yes, Martin moved around and did things. His rolling gait — coupled with his stocky build — was easily recognized from a distance. Up close, his ever-present grin with a flash of white teeth showed in the middle of his beard. His eyes were always alert. He never missed a thing. I always enjoyed talking to him about boats, hot spots to fish, or "Did you hear that Frank got himself a big moose out by mile eighteen?"

I remember the day that Martin yelled over to me as I headed across the dock to the ship's gangplank. "Did you hear that the Alaska Game Commission is offering $150 per head on all of the mountain goats you can catch?"

Well, I had decided a long time ago that I did not want to catch any goats. It turned out that the commission wanted to introduce goats to the Kodiak Islands. The offer had first been made in the Skagway/Haines area with no takers. The big question was, "How does one capture a mountain goat? And, after you've got him, what do you do?"

Martin said, "I'm going to collect as many goats as I can."

It was possibly ten days or two weeks later when I heard that Martin was in the Seward General Hospital. As soon as I could get away from work, I visited him. There he was in bed with his right leg in a cast. I knew that he hadn't been injured on the job. Sure enough, a goat got him. He told me about his plan for capturing goats and what went wrong.

"You see, I got to thinking. All animals in the hilly and mountainous country immediately head for the high ground when they are in danger. Without fail, they have their escape routes and the animals use them. So I went out into an area that I knew and jumped a flock of goats, and observed through my glasses their escape route. The next day, I packed up a chunk of an old seine net and installed it high in a deep part of the chute that the goats use. That afternoon, I started up from down-low and herded the goats into the chute where the net stopped them. I had a length of rope, figuring that I'd somehow snare or tie up at least one goat. I got up close to them—there were four. They weren't tangled up in the net but just leaning back against the net away from me. I stood there wondering what I'd do next, when one of the billies made a dash at me and down I went. I don't know if he hit me or if I just fell over backward. Anyhow, it was very steep and I rattled around a lot before I stopped. Sure enough, I had a broken leg."

I can't imagine how he crawled, hopped, and stumbled down the mountain, but somehow he made it to his pickup. Luckily it was equipped with automatic drive which made driving with one leg a simple thing.

He told me, "I'll be after them next fall, you can be sure."

One year later, after much thought and planning, Martin went after the goats. This time he didn't do it alone. His brother was brought

Mountain goats (left center) on a hillside.

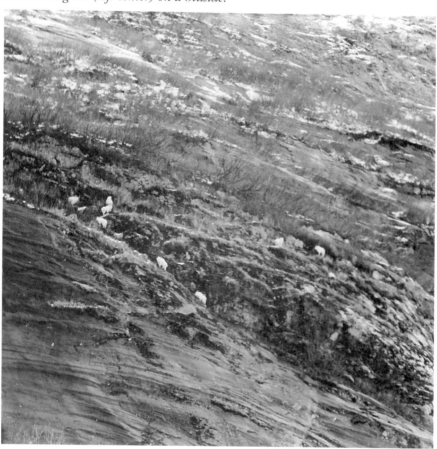

187

into the caper. Armed with fishing net, ropes, and a twelve-foot pole with a loop on the end that could be drawn tight, the goats were no match for the brothers. The goats were captured much like a cowboy bulldogs a steer. With the dangerous sharp pointed horns secured, Martin moved in and hog-tied the feet. It was no little job to carry six goats down the mountain to their truck, but they did it.

While capturing the goats, Martin discovered an odd thing. The animals appeared to be highly emotional. One of the animals was acting up and Martin took a short-handled club and tapped the goat on his horn. Martin made sure that I understood that he hit them lightly. Much to his surprise, the goat fainted, passed-out, or whatever. This turned out to be the standard procedure to calm all of the goats.

The Game Commission flew in and picked up the goats for transportation to Kodiak. Martin was hired to go along for the purpose of keeping the goats quiet.

"That was the easiest money that I ever earned," Martin said. "All I had to do was sit there and tap a goat's horn whenever it woke up or became rowdy."

While with the Alaska Game Commission, and later living in Alaska, I never again heard of this strange behavior of goats. Could it be that nobody has been as close to a goat since Martin?

NOME—
AND A HAPPENING
ALONG THE WAY

Unalakleet and McGrath, 1957

T HE ANNUAL All-Alaska Chamber of Commerce meeting was held in Nome the first week in May 1957. Members from Ketchikan to Kotzebue attended. This was the first visit to Nome for my wife, Ann, and me, so it was with great interest and pleasure that we took in the town and surrounding areas.

I believe that early May was the perfect time to visit. It wasn't cold but we did have snow. The shore ice was still frozen to the beach extending an eighth of a mile or more out to the floating pack-ice that drifted back and forth with the wind and tide. The Eskimo women were fishing through the cracks in the ice while the men were in their oomiaks (skin boats) hunting oogoruk (bearded seal).

The King Island Eskimo village, immediately east of Nome, was of special interest as our oomiaks and dog sleds were pulled up on the beach. Drying racks of seal, walrus, and fish gave us a rare photo opportunity. We saw an old lady outside a tiny shack scooping up dirty snow to be melted for laundry water. Later we caught a glimpse of a young girl in a pure white blouse coming out of the same shack, and we wondered how she could have gotten the blouse so white. At the airport they gave us a "tourist show" of native dances and the blanket toss. The so-called blanket toss consists of walrus skins sewn together. Many eager hands circled the blanket and heaved one person high into the air. This fun activity grew from the original need of the hunters to get a higher outlook to see game. Facing out to sea with the blanket, it is not uncommon to toss someone thirty to thirty-five feet into the air for a lofty view of the area. Despite the tourist show, Nome was still living its normal life before the invasion of the summer tourist.

Blanket toss in the native village.

The Alaska Steamship Company maintained a company office and living quarters for the Nome agent who lived there during the shipping season, and it was here we stayed. Luckily the house was on the ocean side of Front Street, which meant the ground was thawed by the comparatively warm ocean water, providing the luxury of a septic tank. Buildings on the opposite side of the street were on permafrost and had to use honey buckets. Previous to the installation of massive riprap, being on the ocean side was a disadvantage due to the destructive storms.

A sign in the bathroom read, "Is this flush necessary? Each flush cost 25 cents. If it's yellow, let it mellow. If it's brown, flush it down."

During the winter months, the water is trucked in from a spring that flows all year. I was present when a load of water was delivered. The building's water storage tank was installed in the insulated attic. Two pipes led from the tank to the outside ground level. One was the filler pipe and the other was the overflow. The tank truck had an electric pump with a long extension cord. The operator plugged the cord into the house's outlet and, with a flexible coupling, secured his tank to the filler pipe. A stream of water gushing out of the overflow pipe indicated that the tank was full.

Nome is a "white man's" town. No self-respecting Alaska native planning to live off the land would settle on Nome's unprotected beach. For centuries, the people have lived further west on the Seward Peninsula and on King Island and the Little Diomede. Here there is an abundance of birds, seal, walrus, fish, and sometimes whales. After Nome was settled, the King Islanders would paddle their boats the eighty miles to sell their handicrafts and obtain summer employment. In the fall, before the freeze-up, they returned to the island. When the Bureau of Indian Affairs condemned their school, the natives moved en masse to Nome. The men still return to the island during the summer to hunt and gather bird eggs.

The Little Diomede is two miles across the Bering Strait from Russia, which owned Big Diomede. The Cold War restricted visits of family and friends between the islands. Happily, that is not now the case. A look at a map of Alaska might lead you to believe that the St. Lawrence Islands and the Little Diomede are the farthest west of all of North America. However, you might be surprised to learn that Attu, the last island of the Aleutian Island chain, is even slightly west of Christchurch, New Zealand.

During the chamber's meeting, I envied Ann. While I sat in the meeting looking out a picture window toward the ice and sea beyond, I could see Ann out on the ice observing and talking to the natives. There were a number of people who had been patients at the Tuberculosis Sanitarium in Seward, where we were living at the time, and had mutual friends. I recall that at Christmas time each Eskimo patient was given a quart of seal oil as a special gift. That present was much treasured. Turkey dinner received a generous amount of seal oil.

What happened on the way to Nome? Alaska Airlines timed the

inaugural flight of their newest jet plane to fly the Chamber of Commerce members to Nome. The flight was booked to capacity. This was definitely a PR flight and was duly noted in all of the Alaskan newspapers. The group was a happy, friendly crowd of Alaskans out for an adventure. We knew a number of the passengers from previous meetings. In fact, Bob Scott, a friend from our Juneau days, was in the third seat with us on the right side of the plane. The weather was clear and cold. Sunny weather was projected for our flight and we were to have stops at McGrath and Unalakleet before our arrival at Nome.

On the descent into McGrath, the pilot came on the intercom and said, "We will be on the ground a little longer than usual due to the unloading of a large transformer. Plan on forty minutes or longer on the ground."

Everyone deplaned to stretch their legs and have a look around.

McGrath was settled in 1906. It is 226 miles northwest of Anchorage and situated on the Kuskokwim River, directly south of its confluence with the Takotna. Prior to airplanes, the only way to McGrath was from the Bering Sea and Kuskokwim Bay. McGrath is the northern-most accessible point for sternwheelers and riverboats. Of course, if you had cabin fever, you could travel by dog team in the winter to Seward, some 398 miles away. In 1908, the government established a winter trail. By 1911 to 1925, a regular mail and transportation service was used from Seward to Nome, serving Flat, Iditorod, McGrath, and other gold-strike areas. Interestingly enough, one of the responsibilities of the Federal Alaska Road Commission was to keep the dog team trails open and well-marked. This trail is the one still used during the annual dog team race from Anchorage to Nome — called the Iditarod Trail.

Bob Scott, Ann, and I decided to walk east, down the runway to the Kuskokwim River where there was a picturesque log cabin trading post. The land sloped off so the airfield was built up. This created a twenty-five-foot drop to the river. I was surprised to see the river running clear; however, further south, it is a silt-laden stream. The trading post was interesting to see and we were glad that we had taken the walk, rather than hanging around the plane. Ever aware of the time, we headed back to the airfield, planning our arrival a good ten to fifteen minutes ahead of the time of departure. Climbing the incline, we observed a plane taking off to the west. At first we assumed another plane had arrived and departed. No! The plane growing smaller and smaller was ours! McGrath is not a village one would care to overnight. Besides, a big bash was planned for that evening in Nome, hosted by Alaska Airlines.

We rushed to the agent's office and demanded the plane return and pick us up. The agent scoffed, asking, "Do you have any idea how much it would cost for that plane to return for you?"

I countered with, "Have you any idea how much your headquarters will like to read in every Alaskan newspaper from Ketchikan to Kotzebue how through the negligence of your crew, the plane departed twenty minutes early? And how the flight attendants failed to notice three empty seats in a capacity load? You will be the fall-guy unless you let the pilot make the decision. He in turn, can pass the decision on to headquarters if he so desires. May I again recommend that you call the plane."

With that, he went into his office and shut the door. We wondered what he would do. In the meantime, we were watching the small speck in the sky become smaller and smaller. Then, to our amazement and relief, the speck in the sky made a wide turn and returned to McGrath. We hurriedly entered the cabin and were met with loud laughs and cheers. The plane took off immediately.

On the descent into Unalakleet, the pilot came on the intercom advising passengers of the usual things and added, "We will be on the ground a very short time. You may deplane if you wish, but we ask that you remain in the immediate area. We are asking, however, that Mr. Scott and Mr. and Mrs. Jeffrey remain in their seats with their seat belts securely fastened."

Everyone had a big laugh at our expense. Of course we did deplane. Unalakleet is a small Eskimo village on the shore of the Bering Sea. Despite its drab appearance — most of the snow had melted — the good humor of the people was displayed in front of the agent's office. A fenced-off area — possibly two feet by eight feet — had been planted with grass, most likely brought in from the States. A sign read "Keep off the Grass."

Much to our pleasure, the pilot overflew Nome and took us to the Bering Straits. We circled the American Little Diomede Island and then crossed over to the Siberian Big Diomede. The pilot assured us that despite the Cold War, we would not be fired upon if we intruded no further.

That night at the big banquet, we were somewhat celebrities and were pointed out repeatedly. I would guess that there are not too many people who can boast that a big jet has turned around and made a second landing just to pick them up.

A NEW SCHOOL
FOR KONGIGANAK

KONGIGANAK, 1975

THE LAST THING that Ann said prior to dropping me off at the Seattle/Tacoma Airport was, "Don't take any chances. After all, what you are doing is above and beyond the call of your job."

I assured her that I'd take it easy and let the young guys take the chances, knowing full well that there weren't going to be any young guys to do what I had to do.

It all started the day before, September 30, 1975, with a phone call from Jack Anderson in Anchorage. Well, I guess I'd better go back to the beginning.

Our firm, The Northland Marine Line was a tug and barge firm that served Alaska. We had contracted with the Bureau of Indian Affairs to transport a complete school to Kongiganak. You might ask, where is Kongiganak? A very poor joke would be to answer that it is just north of Kwigillingok. Most Alaskan maps do not show this village. If one goes down the Kuskokwim River from Bethel over a hundred miles to the Kuskokwim Bay and the Bering Sea, you'll find both Kongiganak and Kwigillingok.

Well, our regular equipment was already in use, so it was necessary to use someone else's services. Thus, the firm formed a towing arrangement with Jack Anderson. The school on board the barge was prepackaged to make helicopter lifts from the barge to the village of Kongiganak. Everything was simple and there were going to be no problems. The BIA assured us they would determine where the tug and barge would lay at anchor during the discharge. They knew that the place of anchorage required a minimum of twelve feet of water at low water of zero tide.

"No problem," they said. "Our people will come up with the answer."

That's why Jack's call to me was a bombshell. The BIA had not followed through with their commitment for assistance and Andy Anderson, Jack's son, understandably refused to go north of Goodnews Bay with the tow until these answers were found:

1. Who was the Kuskokwim Bay pilot and where would Andy meet him?
2. After arriving in the river, who would be the pilot to take Andy back down to the anchorage?
3. Last and definitely the most important, where will the ultimate destination be? Will there be twelve feet of water at low tide throughout the discharge? Who says there is that much water and how do they know?

"After all, this tug is new and worth a lot of bucks on the end of the towline and we can't trust the word of some muskrat hunter who needs only enough water for his skiff and outboard motor!" Jack Anderson explained. "I'm sorry, Jeff, you're stuck with this problem. I've already done a lot of calling to the BIA and Bethel with no progress at all."

This operation was already a month late, due to a delayed arrival of the cargo and the time that it took for special packaging. Our concern now was that ice and total freeze-up in shallow, fresh water generally occurred in October. If everything failed, I figured that we could deliver the shipment to Bethel in the spring of 1976. But this would only be our last resort. Ole Sumstad, the Bay and River pilot whom I first knew nineteen years ago when he was sailing first mate on the *M.V. Susitna*, got on the phone to me and said, "Jack, you'd better grab the first airplane you can get and get up here in a hurry."

It is certainly true that it isn't what you know but whom you know in Alaska that is important. That is why I was on the early flight to Anchorage with a connection to Bethel.

My connection at Anchorage was good, and with the change of time, my arrival in Bethel was just in time for lunch at the Kuskokwim Café. The wind gusted at about 20 to 30 mph and the air was quite chilly. It was freezing at night but the temperature rose above 32°F when the sun came out. Jimmy Hoffman wasn't in the office and I could see that Ole's pilot boat was anchored in the river. I yelled and waved but couldn't raise anyone. A twelve-year-old Indian boy was racing around in his outboard skiff, so I hired him for a buck to ferry me out to Ole's boat.

Ole's wife was a native as was his crew. They all crowded around while we discussed what should be done. Ole told me that he and his crew knew a lot about the area and that they were quite sure that the creeks at Kongiganack and Kwigillingok were far too shallow to lay at anchor. Ole also explained that the creeks twisted and turned at such an extent that there was absolutely no way that a barge of our size could make the corners. Frankly, they didn't know where a good anchorage was. We discussed whom to use for the bar pilot and another pilot if we needed to head toward Kongiganak. Both men lived in the villages that I was to investigate. We hailed the kid in the skiff again, and he earned another buck.

Jimmy Hoffman was in his office upon my return. He formerly flew for Wein Airlines after he quit bush flying, so he was definitely the one to talk to regarding flyers.

It was really quite simple, Jimmy told me. "Frankly, the weather is so lousy, especially the wind, that nobody is flying. The weather report says that it will continue to be cold and windy. However, if the wind drops some, there is one flyer that I know who just might fly for you. He knows the country down there and can speak the language, too."

Jimmy made a call. By the time I'd finished my second cup of coffee, my pilot arrived. He was a native, about twenty-five years old with a face scarred up with two-week-old cuts. He gave me a big, toothless smile at our introduction.

"What happened to you?" I asked.

197

"Oh, I busted up a plane and banged my face into the instrument panel."

With that said, he agreed to fly in the morning if the wind dropped. Yes, he knew the area and the people very well. I discussed with him what had to be done. I explained that I had to find an anchorage and "sound" it around low water time. We covered the subject as best that we could, guessing what we would be up against, and parted. The tide was low at 11 A.M. on October 2, reading 0.2 feet. We'd depart as soon after daybreak as possible.

Arriving at the inn, I was pleased to see Jim Lepage. Jim was with our firm and was out beating the bush for business. Word had been sent out for him to join me and assist wherever possible. It was great to have somebody with me, even if it was just for company. Over a drink we discussed the drill to implement should a suitable spot to sound be discovered. After dinner I made a sounding line out of rope and old pipe couplings. Luckily, I also rigged up two eight-feet-long sticks and bound them together so that I could slide them out and have a 14-foot sounding stick. With that, I went to bed and dreamed of many wild situations with my toothless pilot.

Properly clothed for cold weather, we arrived at the river prior to daylight. Our pilot was already there, roping off the wings. That is, he was scraping off the frost. We didn't discuss the wind gusts, so I guessed that we were going to fly. After pumping gallons of water out from the pontoons and warming up the engine, we took off. It was a wild, bouncy ride all the way! The flight lasted about one hour. The delta at low water was mostly sand bars, with channels here and there. Once across the bar coming north we could see a channel leading southwest toward Kongiganak. Yes, with the tide in we would need a pilot here, too, or so I thought. We made a couple of passes over Kongiganak and Kwigillingok and knew immediately that the creeks were far too small, shallow, and crooked for our purpose. Coming down I had spotted a fair-sized inlet that my chart indicated as the Ishkowish River. The chart did not show any sounding, however. It was six to seven miles from Kongiganak, and would be suitable to our use if it had enough water.

Over the noise of the engine, I asked the pilot if he could land and take off inside the inlet. Timing with his stopwatch, we made a pass upwind and one downwind. He yelled at me, "With this wind, we can do it. With no wind, it is too tight."

I pointed down and down we went. Luck was with us that day. The wind was from the west, which was the long-ways of the little bay. Once on the water and with the power chopped, there was hardly any advance against the wind. At once it became apparent that we would only be able to sound upwind. The pilot would have to keep a good amount of power on to keep steerage-way. So Jim and I went into our act.

I climbed out of the righthand door and stood on the pontoon. I had some protection from the wind and the propeller wash standing behind the door, but the waves splashing over the floats and the water driven off the prop did a quick job of soaking me through. A couple of casts with my makeshift sounding line proved to be a bust. The door, wind, and the wings' struts made it impossible to cast the line ahead for a proper sounding. Then I remembered that I had in fact brought along the 8-foot sticks and lashed them to the floats. I secured them together making a 14-foot probe. With Jim hanging on to my belt so I wouldn't fall, we went up and down the inlet, sounding. Much to my surprise, I did not reach bottom even close in to the south bank. However, when we taxied near the river mouth, it got down to seven or eight feet. Obviously, this spot was our safe anchorage.

I gave the stick a big heave and yelled, "Head for Bethel!"

As we left, I figured that Andy would come in on high tide having at least seventeen feet at the inlet's entrance. Once inside, he would have plenty of water even with a minus tide.

The flight back was fun as we bounced around flying over the little villages of Eek, Kuskovak, Tuntutuliak, Eenayarak, Napaskiak, and Napakiak. It didn't seem possible, but we were back in Bethel for lunch. It had taken us one hour down, one hour sounding and flying around, and one hour back. It felt like we had been gone for many more hours.

I changed out of my wet clothing and, after lunch, we switched to a wheeled plane and flew to Kwigellingok. Ole had given me a name of a fellow who had worked for him and could pilot the tug across the bar into the Kuskokwim River. The government had constructed small runways for both villages. It seemed like we had just enough room for the landing and takeoff. With the help of our flyer, who could speak the native language, thirty minutes was all it took to nail down the bar pilot. A short jump over to Kongiganak nailed down the man who would lead the tow from the river to the anchorage. It was a few minutes after 4 P.M. and getting dark when we again arrived at Bethel. It seemed unbelievable that so much had been accomplished in one day.

I called Jack Anderson. The first thing that I asked him was, "Do you trust me?"

He replied, "Why, I sure do."

"Well," I said, "here is the information that you and Andy need, and it's all good news."

Jack was surprised and pleased. Andy would be notified to keep coming and Jim LePage would fly the pilot down.

Calls were made to the helicopter people and our Seattle office alerted them that the barge would be in the Ishkowish River on the afternoon tide of October 5. The barge workers and the helicopters were ordered to be in Bethel on the evening of the 5th. Discharge of the new school for Konkiganak was to begin with daylight on the 6th.

I returned to Seattle on October 3rd and was back to work the morning of the 4th. It was one of the fastest and most rewarding trips that I had ever made. As I am writing this story down I can still vividly recall sounding with that stick, the roar of the engine, waves splashing over the floats, and the wind and the propeller wash buffeting me about with Jim hanging on to my belt. You know — it was kind of fun!

ICED TEA, PLEASE!

BETHEL, 1975

I T WAS a clear, beautiful day in June. Bethel is situated on the Kuskokwim River about 102 miles upriver from salt water. The area south of the village (downriver) was a flat lowland with marshes. In fact, despite the distance from the mouth of the river, the tide affected the height of the water at Bethel. The only road within 200 miles or more is the four-mile stretch to the airport. When the locals feel like taking a ride, they zip out to the airport. I always got a kick out of a sign on the left side of the road. Some "wag" transported an evergreen tree to treeless Bethel and planted it alongside the road. As you approach the tree, the sign reads "You Are Now Entering the Bethel National Forest" and after passing the tree, another sign states "You Are Now Leaving the Bethel National Forest."

Until the coming of the white man, Bethel did not exist. The natives lived downriver in the lowlands, where beaver and muskrats abounded and where they could hunt for fur and meat. Fish, of course, were plentiful. Others lived upriver in the higher country, where moose and caribou were there for the taking. Bethel became the trading hub. I suppose the population was 75 percent Indian and 25 percent Eskimo, with possibly seventy-five or fewer whites.

It was here that the deep-water vessels unloaded their cargo. Freight for upriver destinations was unloaded and forwarded on shallow draft vessels. For years the Alaska Steamship Company, using a specialized vessel, operated upriver to Bethel. The rule was that the ship could not draw more than twenty-feet to negotiate the river bar and make it upstream. Large ocean-going barges and tugs have now replaced the ships.

We had a loaded barge due at Bethel in two days. I was the advance man for our cargo-working crew. The crew was in Anchorage on "R &R" after working a barge at Dillingham. My job at that time was to make arrangements for housing and feeding the men plus the final plans of discharge.

Much to my surprise, it was hot. Of course it wouldn't have been quite so warm had we been wearing our state-side summer clothing. The clerk at the Kuskokwim Inn told me, "The worst part of the heat is that last week's mosquitoes, this week's, and next week's all hatch out at the same time."

Yes, I had noticed the little devils. In fact, I had a large bag full of Cutter's spray to use myself and to give to the crew. The Indians and Eskimos swore by it and that was good enough for me. Prior to dressing in the morning, standing in shorts and T-shirt, the men took turns spraying all exposed flesh—this included neck and hair. Then we rubbed the stuff onto our hands and carefully applied it to the face without touching the eyes or forehead. Sweating on the forehead results in burning eyes. At work, every man had a can of Cutter's in his back pocket, just in case.

My first trip to Bethel didn't live up to my expectations. In fact, I hoped I would never have to go there ever again. The village was wide open. Bars and liquor stores were open on a twenty-four-hour basis. There was drunkenness in evidence everywhere. I was especially saddened early one morning watching an eight-year-old girl leading her drunk grandmother home after an all-night binge.

The Indian Chief of Police told me, "Conditions are really bad. We believe the children suffer the most, as they are unattended much of the time, poorly clothed and poorly fed. But Alaska provided for local autonomy regarding liquor sales." He went on to explain that the fall's election would most likely be carried by the Methodists."

In Alaska, any group favoring liquor and gambling restrictions at that time were referred to as Methodists.

"If the Methodists win," he added, "the sale of liquor will be prohibited."

The following spring I was pleased to see the children well-clothed and fed. Yes, the bars and liquor stores were boarded up. Upon seeing me, the chief said, with pride, "Now, how do you like our village?"

The villages downriver have some tongue-twister-type names like Kwingillinguk, Akulurak, and Napakiak. An easier one to pronounce for us non-natives, is Aniak. The river is open to navigation up to McGrath, which is due west of Mt. Mckinley.

It was after lunch, so I took a hike to the Kuskokwim Cafe. I passed a number of sled dogs chained outside their houses. The poor things were about mad from insect bites. All of their muzzles, noses, eyes, and ears were bloody. I felt so sorry for them. Having protected myself with Cutter's, I was in fine shape. There was a solid door into the café that was open to provide ventilation. A screen door had been installed to ward off the onslaught of the ever-present mosquito. In fact, they were so thick, I couldn't see into the café but I could hear their steady drone.

A voice from inside said, "Give the door a number of shakes and bangs and then come in — in a hurry."

I was surprised at how few insects entered with me. The voice turned out to be the only customer. He pointed at a chair, and said, "I'm lonesome. Come and have lunch with me. I haven't even looked at the menu."

As it turned out, he was in charge of the firefighters and smoke jumpers dispatched to fight the fires on the tundra that had been started by lightning strikes.

"You know," he said, "while I've been out on the fire line in the heat and smoke, I've worked up a big thirst for a huge glass of iced tea."

Gosh, I thought, I don't ever recall hearing of anyone in Alaska drinking iced tea. Hmmm, not in Nome, Anchorage, Juneau, or Ketchikan. Maybe, just maybe, some weird person unbeknownst to me, has had iced tea, but I doubted it. This guy was from Idaho.

The native waitress finally came out of the kitchen to take our order. When my friend ordered iced tea, I watched her face. She must have been a good poker player because this strange order didn't seem to faze her. She remained in the kitchen for an unusually long time. Finally, she returned to our table and said, "We have four kinds of cold beer, Coca-Cola, Seven-Up, and root beer. Would you care for any of those?"

"No," he said. "I have my heart set on iced tea. Please, iced tea."

Our orders, at long last, arrived. The last item to be placed on the table was a tall glass of ice water and a tea bag. He looked at me and asked, "Is this the way? Will it work?"

I didn't know. Holding the string of the tea bag, he dunked it up and down, up and down, at least twenty times. The ice water, very slightly, changed color. Next, he experimented with banging the tea bag around in the glass with a spoon with very little success. Finally, he took a sip and said, "Well, at least it's cold."

I've since learned how to make iced tea with hot water and also sun tea. I bet he has, too.

TROUT FISHING —
A LETTER TO DREW

DILLINGHAM AND ILIAMNA LAKE

Jack and his sister, Helen, in North Dakota. Fishing started young for Jack.

Dear Drew,

I have a copy of your essay on fly fishing. I think it is very good. I, also understand that you are an accomplished fly tier.

When I was your age, living in northwestern North Dakota, no one seemed to know about fly fishing. We used short poles and a cork on the line to keep the hook off of the bottom. On the Missouri River, we used overnight set lines anchored out in the current.

In Alaska, I saw my first fly fisherman. Wow, I thought, that's for me. After I caught everything behind me, including my hat, I gave up and mostly trolled for salmon. However, since you are a fisherman, I'd like to tell you about the most wonderful rainbow trout fishing that I ever had.

We were living in Juneau, Alaska. I was with the Alaska Game Commission at the time. In the spring of 1939, I was directed to go to the Bristol Bay area to assist the Wildlife Agent with the spring beaver sealing. I took a passenger ship from Juneau to Seward across the Gulf of Alaska. Then, I rode the Alaska Railroad passenger train to Anchorage. My passage from Anchorage to Dillingham was to be the next day by a small nine-passenger plane equipped with skis. Although the snow was all gone in Anchorage, it still looked like winter in Bristol Bay. There was no airfield at Dillingham, but the plane could land on snow in any open area or land on the ice on the Nushagak River. We made three attempts to fly through the mountain passes, as at that time the airplanes were not capable of flying high enough to go over the mountains, but each time it was snowing and blowing and the pilot could not see his way. So, I stayed in Anchorage and helped around the commission's office.

It was then that I met Gren Collins, who will be the "star" of this story. Gren had just arrived in Anchorage after spending one year up in Arctic Alaska with the Eskimos. Wainwright (southwest of Barrow), Barrow, and many small settlements east of Barrow on the Beaufort Sea were his working area. He went "native" to the extent that he could work, eat, and live like a native. He had his own plane and he invited me to come along for a ride to "get out of the smell of the office." After living in the "sticks" for so long, an office was too confining for him. It was a fun ride until he said, "As long as we are up here, would you mind if we landed at the airport rather than return to the lake?" Hey, wait a minute, I thought, we are on skis and the airport is 100 percent dry, snowless gravel." I replied, "Sure, why not?" I learned later that the ice was expected to go out soon, and Gren didn't have floats for his plane but he would go to wheels. So, down we went. At touchdown, Gren raised the nose, and applied enough power to sort of hang the plane in a stall. The skis made a terrible noise on the gravel. On the ground, but still moving ahead, he cut the throttle. The plane lunged ahead and broke the prop, but it didn't flop onto its back. Whew, we were down, and safe. Gren said, "I did it. I thought I could land this baby on dry ground, and I did." Was I scared? Are you kidding?

But, back to fishing. Johnny Walotca, a well-known bush pilot, and Gren were great friends. One day, I went along with Johnny in his Bristol Bay Air Service plane on a U.S. Mail and freight run to

Jack fly fishing up the Taku River, within four miles of Canada. Good trout fishing, but note the mosquito net over his hat!

Dillingham. It was spring and the plane had been switched to floats. Johnny confirmed that the weather was great so the flight was a "go," and the plane was loaded to capacity. I got to ride up front with Johnny.

The flight through the mountain passes was pretty but kind of scary. Halfway up one pass, an eastbound plane zipped over us. (Gosh, I thought, during the snowstorms when we were in this same pass I wouldn't have liked to meet another plane at the same altitude.)

Past the mountains, we continued to fly southwest over a huge lake named Iliamna. Johnny yelled over the noise of the engine, "How would you like to fish in possibly the best trout fishing river in the world? I doubt if over twenty people have ever fished in this isolated spot." "Gosh," I said. "Sure, but I don't have boots, nor fishing gear." Johnny came back with, "No problem, I have extra everything. Oh, and Gren is right behind us and will join us for the fun." You know, those darn guys had planned this all along, I thought.

Much to my surprise, we landed on the lake and grounded the floats on a sandy shore. Gren secured his plane a short distance from us. I couldn't imagine where this fishing stream could be.

In no time, we were outfitted. I followed Johnny. The stream wasn't over a

Jack with his rainbow trout at Iliamna Lake.

hundred yards from the lake's beach. It paralleled the beach for approximately 300 yards before joining the lake. The stream was alive with fish. Johnny said, "The smaller fish are red salmon up here to spawn. The bigger fish are rainbow trout up  here to eat the salmon eggs. We use barbless hooks with a red bead above the hook. Every fish caught is released without injury. This is fun fishing. We, usually, wager a dollar as to who lands the first fish. It doesn't count if you yell "I got one" or if you say nothing. The winner must say, "I have a rain- bow trout." I thought the rule was a little weird, but what the heck? I believe I made twelve casts before I didn't get a strike. Bringing those fighters to the net was something else.

Gren landed the first trout. He held that thrashing fish in his hands and said, "You are so beautiful." With that, he held it up high and then brought it to his mouth, and took a big bite out of its left side. "Ah," he said, "That's mighty fine eating."

It was then that I remembered that Glen had lived with the Eskimos, and ate whale, seal, and fish — raw.

Jack Jeffrey

210